A
Schizoid
at
Smith

A
Schizoid
at
Smith

How Overparenting Leads to Underachieving

Blair Sorrel

atmosphere press

Published by Atmosphere Press

Cover design by Ronaldo Alves

Cover photo by Seymour Sheldon
The author and Army Nurse Gertrude Shapiro, photographed in 1944 on the Island
of Tinian in the Marianas Group. Shapiro was later part of the first medical landing
group in Hiroshima after the atomic bomb was dropped. Photo donated by Rita
Sharon. National Museum of American Jewish Military History: Women in the
Military: A Jewish Perspective. The National Museum of American Jewish Military
History, 1811 R Street N.W. Washington, D.C. 20009

atmospherepress.com

"Ah, look at all the lonely people!"
Paul McCartney, Lennon-McCartney, *Eleanor Rigby*

Preface

"I guess you wonder how you got to where you are?" said Selma Landisberg, Clinician, July 1988. This was the opening gambit in our first session of a lengthy, very pivotal relationship.

A memoir answers that existential query by recounting and embellishing life experiences.

"If I had your life, I would want to forget all about it," my father muttered, adding, "Heartbreaking. You had so much hardship," then shaking his head allowed, "I don't want you to go through it anymore."

Fast-forward. I sat mostly mute in a Memoir Writing course at CUNY Graduate Center in 2000. I penned not a single word throughout the duration of the semester. After one class, a kind participant approached me, "I wish you would contribute more as I find your comments so insightful."

The elderly instructors both nodded, assuring me that one day I would definitely tell my story. What did they see in me that I didn't?

Memoirs are for superachievers, hobnobbers, and globetrotters with exotic opportunities and destinations. Mine had been a marginal subsistence fraught with rejection and despair. A homeless person with a roof over her head and a resident cat family.

In spite of all projections to the contrary at Smith College, I grossly underachieved in every key area—I had no employment stability, career, boyfriend, or marriage on the horizon, and I was longer in the tooth.

"I knew right away you suffered from withdrawal when I heard about all the jobs, the way you spoke, and from the testing, none of which was grounded in reality," Selma would later impart. Whereupon she dusted the *Diagnostic and Statistical Manual of Mental Illness* and read the descriptors of schizoid personality disorder: desire to be alone, have difficulty expressing emotions, may seem humorless or cold, have trouble holding jobs...

"Does any of this sound like you?"

"Those sound like drifters!" I burst out, aghast.

"Too bad you hadn't entered therapy sooner, you would have had less trauma," she resigned. So this begs the question...

a memoir about this mess. Who would want to read such a work?

Theologian and philosopher, Teilhard de Chardin wrote (much more eloquently) that the trick in life is to take anything bad and turn it into something good.

Since so little is known about this disorder, the population scarcely presents, and the afflicted are usually male, I decided to come out of the cupboard and shed light on this arcane condition. My firm hope is to preclude others from enduring what I had, to offer help to the silent sufferers—their therapists, teachers, and family members, and to instill greater societal tolerance toward people of any difference.

"If you remember the '60's, you weren't really there." is a familiar baby boomer adage attributed to many. I wasn't all there then and even occasionally now. I have done my best to reconstruct this selective vision of an enshrined era. And yes, it took all of the '70's and well beyond for me to recover from that turbulence and from the nefarious imprint of over-parenting that I experienced beginning at age five.

Chapter 1

Imprinted by Five

It was Saturday night, and the tinny echo of canned laughter reverberated from the Zenith round screen TV in our understated living room. This spacious apartment above my father's ophthalmological practice in Ball Square was spare but welcoming. The windows fronted Broadway, and I could wave to him as he went to work, although he merely exited one doorway and entered another below. How I anticipated Daddy's return, after seemingly endless hours. Even though he was usually quite fatigued, he was always still ready with a weary smile and hug.

Meals were a tacit ritual, after which he would crumple onto his twin bed in the master bedroom. His nap would segue within seconds into a heavy slumber. Our tabby skittered in the chiaroscuro shadows. The diminutive screen's raucous voices couldn't quell my dread of the dark. Needing Daddy but knowing he was dozing and still craving care, I fumbled in the ombre surroundings of the hallway, now transformed into a cold, cavernous space.

A bright beacon emanated from the slightly ajar bathroom door. I shambled toward it to say good night, but felt the sting of a goodbye slap instead. "Beat it." It was our mercurial nanny, Mary, who wanted her privacy instead. Why did Mommy leave us girls with her so often?

My mother was a Women's Army Auxiliary Corps or WAAC nurse during World War II, stationed in the major Pacific Theater. Her training never eluded our family. Even during peacetime, we all remained on high alert as her stern warnings readied us for battle, be it in the field or in the bathroom.

"Invisible, menacing growths pervaded a lavatory. Utilizing a toilet seat in public," she admonished, "could precipitate something far worse, an evil entity known as germs, an ominous growth that would eventually overtake my tiny form."

Growths? I tried to reconcile the colorful profusion of perennials and annuals that graced the small yard outside, wondering how anything so lovely could portend such insidious, interior danger. Never mind, soon, I would be sheltered from this hazard in a safe haven.

Ah, summer camp, the rustic charm of white cabins with forest green shutters situated in bucolic surroundings. This inviting communal living would provide a heartening home away from home experience and a dream hiatus.

Yet people would be there. And for a schizoid, strangers and socializing are always unsettling no matter how enticing the setting.

Little accompanied me on this adventure besides my pastel

suitcase and trepidation. My bedwetting made sleepovers even at a relative's daunting. Awaiting a cot assignment, I could only hope for the bottom bunk and a short sprint to the water closet—lest I lie anguished, chagrined in my dank, fetid nightie, and now sodden institutional sheets.

Night terrors, thrashing around in bed, a urinous high dive in the gloaming. This nocturnal sequence would give an entirely new meaning to being caught with your pants down. How mortifying if my bunkmates were still wide awake. Would this vignette become a winceable camp recollection years from now, the kind of lore that would impel my parents to move out of state?

Maybe the nubile, young counselor would also chastise me in front of all the others? How could I explain my incontinence to them? Would I be expelled? *Perhaps you'll be lucky, and they'll sleep through the whole drill,* I nervously surmised. *Just adhere to the toilet training that my mother had assured me would prepare me for the outside world.* Personal hygiene was, after all, paramount to our life lessons.

And most critical to the protocol, was never, ever sitting on that shared toilet. This last precept differentiated me at Pembroke Summer Camp. I suddenly found myself in a one-on-one conference with its director, Hadassah Blocker, who insisted on knowing not only the how of this idiosyncrasy, but the why. She called for me to make a dry run. I merely reiterated the inculcation endured in my household; a ménage known among my peers as *The Addams Family.*

The world, according to my mother Gertrude, had its own rule book. Perching on a boulder may induce a bladder infection. Only touch the business end of a surface or doorknob. Fingerprints besmirched a home. Make every trip matter. Never split an infinitive, or commit any other grammatical faux pas whenever possible. Wearing blue and black in the same outfit is strictly prohibited. Leaving a book open would disfigure its spine. Pronouncing the "l" in almond betrayed ignorance. "Say it, don't spray it! Modulate your voice," and Lady Macbeth, "...What's done cannot be undone."

No nicknames were to be uttered within earshot; she loathed being called Trudy or Gert, so I understood. Slurring words in a street smart fashion was not to be condoned in this elitist domicile.

Beyond our ivory tower, my consciousness clicked like a Polaroid Swinger Land Camera capturing groupings in their environs every ten seconds. "Swing it up, it says yes," froze images of clans laughing and luxuriating in each other's company.

At a cursory glimpse, other parents seemed to allow their children to be children, learn from their mistakes, and consume hearty fare. My culinary-challenged mother (a trait I inherited) eschewed all domestic responsibilities as too lowbrow and tedious to abide. She had wed my father's office, and their union was a loveless partnership. No public or private displays of affection for any of us.

Her Sisterhood acquaintances admired her artistry, her lively mind, and her unconventional mien, but maybe less if they knew the behind-the-scenes. Dr. Spock, the patron saint of mothers of that era and well beyond, convinced them that they were well equipped for the demands. Parenting, for all its extreme responsibility, has no licensing. Stricter requirements and testing exist for driving a car.

"We all came home, and we all had children. There was no advice. We didn't know anything about child-rearing. No one knew. It was supposed just to happen," *Look Magazine's* Senior Editor, George Leonard, commented on his contemporaries' shortcomings, (*Who Created the Baby Boomer Generation and Why* by David Hoffman).

As aging post-war singletons, their vows may have sated their parents' wish for grandchildren, especially during the high birth rate. For the time and tide, they truly appeared a prosaic doctor and nurse couple.

Separate outings with my father to the Morgan Memorial Goodwill store where he foraged, his beloved poking around, for camera parts and tools typified lighthearted and laidback. This revered emporium was a musty, dusty stockpile of new and secondhand merchandise. My clothes were often hand-me-downs, and my toys were mostly salvaged or mongo. Rummaging in bargain bins was our realm rather than posh retail. In fact, many years elapsed before I realized that Filene's had an upstairs. We were truly on the vanguard, a clan of scavengers before it became environmentally friendly.

My stomach growled rapaciously whatever the hour or locale, my appetite increasingly implacable. My vehement cries for "More chicken, more soup!" made me a candidate for an early education foodie's outpost of Overeaters Anonymous. "See how the others eat," my mother would retort and doled out helpings with about the same generosity she proffered tenderness. Mommy's intellectualism definitely got in the way of goofiness or the distinct possibility of gluttony on self-medicating junk food. Local departures into Boston provided a glance into the diverse lives of doting families or cultural differences.

Cloistered in our regimented, austere enclave, we had no inkling of other races. Our lily-white upbringing didn't prepare me for an alien contingent whose swarthy skin prompted me to proclaim excitedly, "Look, there are Hershey's Chocolate people!"

Sharing a cottage in Rocky Neck was the closest semblance of a *Saturday Evening Post* cover for this toddler. Living in proximity to the rustic artists' shacks flanking glinting ocean palettes was paradisal. My mother appeared upbeat, liberated from the welter of paperwork that subsumed her usual days. Frolicking in the sun and surf were beyond majestic diversions for me. Nevertheless, our Cape Ann escapes were not entirely picture-perfect. I still recall making a dash for my flip-flops in the middle of the night as a multiple-alarm fire broke out, sweeping the brittle dwellings as we piled into the wood paneled station wagon for safety.

Speaking of keeping the home fires burning, when Pillsbury's Poppin' Fresh championed, "Nothin' says lovin' like something from the oven," he didn't have my mother or Peg (of the *I Hate to Cook Book*) Bracken in mind. Norman Rockwell could paint a homey dessert the likes of which neither could bake. At potluck dinners, Gertrude's successively singed blueberry tarts became their own version of Table Talk ("America's Favorite Pie") as Gloucester tongues would gag.

In the Eisenhower era, parents just let 'em play, and rug rats were often left unchaperoned, running amuck on the jungle gyms, teeter-totters, seesaws, and other outdoor equipment. Standing in the blazing sun on a base of concrete or asphalt, with rickety wooden fixtures and corroding steel beams, it's a wonder there weren't actual fatalities. Ankle biters often suffered bruises, splinters, tumbles, and burns, but it was all in the name of good fun.

Climbing in a skirt was not as demure as swinging, which was also meant to improve spatial perception. Reaching new heights was invigorating, and I hardly encouraged a youth to position me on the bench and pitch me higher and higher. But the thrill soon left me increasingly disoriented, after recovering from a few vertiginous moments. Unsupervised, the playground was pandemonium, a chaotic swirl of schoolchildren and contraptions, and in my stupefaction, I failed to notice a fast-moving eye level projectile, a seat, headed straight for me.

I blacked out, awakening with a number of stitches smack dab in the center of my forehead. An unmistakable stigma, the incipient price I paid for my continual fantasy life, the only tactic I could mount against overwhelming maternal reprimands. My head was wounded inside and out. A literally marked girl and then woman for the rest of my life.

Navigating a playground wasn't the only dare. The impairment of social withdrawal caused me trouble with many mundane tasks most take for granted: learning to tell time, tie my shoelaces, or even filing in line. My well-meaning father lettered my saddle shoes left and right, as that's how easily addled I could become. On one occasion, a vexed kindergarten teacher smacked me and called me "Nitwit!" in front of the other children for my seeming inability to remain in the queue or descend the staircase in formation.

Daydreaming, possibly thinking about lunch, often distinguished me as an outlander during my lessons. Occasionally irascible teachers conferred the outstanding pupil distinction, that is, the grade school wordplay for out standing in the hallway. My disruptive behavior would now be better construed as hyperactivity.

With my mop of flyaway hair, the bane of my mother's inexorable grooming efforts, some future punks coined me Sheepdog, an easy target—as the shy offer no riposte to bullies. Those more clement probably also derogated me as the black sheep of the schoolyard. Ostracism for pariahs does, indeed, begin during recess. "They don't understand. You're different," my dad would shrug.

"She is always alone," Louisa, a life-sized Mattel doll, sniffed as if I were an insignificant barnacle affixed to the cafeteria table. Although her snarky observation smarted, this cipher remained close-mouthed, simply pining for elsewhere. The outcast reputation officially launched.

When I wasn't being picked on in the schoolyard, my parents *kvetched* that I picked up on things slowly, with mediocre report cards. Mother had a remedial plan. No child of hers, particularly the one that most closely resembled her, would ever be an elementary school malingerer, so she took matters into her own hands and started doing my homework. Even years later, as a freshman at Smith College, I could not compose an essay by myself and took writing tutorials.

Terms of endearment didn't come easily for my mother. Sneak face, bitch, and wastrel were still meant to be motivators. As Gertrude pored over paperwork, my Model T1816R babysitter, a constantly running black and white TV, provided much-needed escapism and fueled my fertile imagination. My newly discovered companions were cartoon characters and sitcoms. Tranquil housekeeping appeared in periodic commercial interruptions with gorgeous wives; perfectly coiffed, attired, manicured, and made up. These exemplars genuinely existed to kowtow to their handsome husbands and telegenic little ones.

In stark contrast, my mother's domestic aversion spewed overwrought hyperbole and histrionics. She was a drama queen decades before the pejorative became popular vernacular. I had difficulty envisioning any of the mothers on the television tucking in her febrile child, boring down to take a temperature, and intoning, "Prepare to die." Not exactly the bedside manner Dr. Spock would advise.

When the spirit moved her, Gertrude had me tag along as she ricocheted among acquaintances. At a neighboring pool party, my eyes gravitated to the lush black Muscat grapes glistening on a patio table. Cezanne would have grabbed a canvas and painted this sensuous still life.

Engrossed and suppressing the urge to lunge for the seemingly forbidden fruit, the gruff host Mr. Katz observed my predilection but also recognized my diffidence. "We will turn our backs so you may eat as many as you like," he mediated with Solomonic wisdom.

When my father, Sydney, tried to introduce me at Sunday School, I managed to vanish in his chinos. "She's bashful," he would explain. Miscast as the Statue of Liberty for a minor holiday performance and having so many ogle me was hellish. The lumbering dowager school marm's breath could peel paint. Her pronouncements castigated my total lack of stage presence, my rounded shoulders, timorous mumble, and vigorous refusal to make eye contact with the audience, as "walking on eggshells."

Suffering for art also necessitated mandatory classical piano lessons at home. My tutor rued that I was more preoccupied with his dandruff and outmoded attire than with learning scales and chords. Not academic, not cool in school, not coordinated or musically inclined, my sense of estrangement augmented. I joined the ranks of card-carrying observers in the plush seclusion of my corner: with its companionable books, cats, and carbohydrates. While catty-corner and at arm's length, were your cooks, brats, and mates.

Also possibly in this silent minority, was America's most renowned and prolific poet, Emily Dickinson. The Belle of Amherst composed a prodigious 1800 poems in forty handbound volumes. Aside from eleven poems, the preponderance of her illustrious creativity would have disappeared had her prescient family not published these works posthumously. Emily Brontë preferred the comradeship of canines. Albert Einstein was an indisputable genius except when it came to social smarts. Pure conjecture, but these notables may have qualified. High achievement is possible in isolation, but the stricken do not seek the limelight. Calmer wallflowers will be fine in mixed company sitting at a safe remove simply staring. The garden variety, like myself, with severe social anxiety, can't concentrate in the presence of others and will probably languish, maybe plummet into homelessness. Lacking competence through inattention, subpar interpersonal skills, and an inappropriate demeanor, they will not conform to corporate culture or performance expectations. Some do manage much better in more solitary occupations like janitorial or lab work, but they generally prefer to function below their capabilities than in a competitive team structure. In truth, of all character disorders, schizoids have about the lowest quality of life predictors as they can barely labor, let alone have careers, seldom date or marry, and usually retain only one close friend or confidant. "You're better off out of an office with this," Thelma Schapiro of the New York State Office of Disability advised at midlife and after a number of years of failure.

Blocked from intimacy, by definition, hinders seeking therapeutic intervention even though this could spare them untold upheaval, possibly their lives. A few may eventually desire treatment for an allied condition or comorbidity, like depression. "This is the least diagnosed personality disorder in the general population, and is uncommon in clinical settings," according to Lumen Learning.

What unifies us autonomous loners is that we are all in a lot of pain but don't know why.

Chapter 2

An Alternative Tale of White Flight

My fifth year on this planet coincided with two watershed events. The much-awaited outset of the progressive John F. Kennedy incumbency, fondly referred to as The Camelot Era. The camera adored picturing the country's charismatic, youngest ever president and his fashion plate wife, Jacqueline, in many official and serendipitous poses. The nation delighted in their leisure activities at their Cape Cod Hyannis Compound or even watching their winsome tots prance in the White House. Their arrival heralded a refreshing new climate, displacing the dowdiness of its former occupants, Dwight and Mamie Eisenhower, and auguring a new wave of liberalism with optimism.

Don't let it be forgot, that once, there was a spot, for one brief, shining moment, that was known as Camelot. "There'll be great presidents again...but there will never be another Camelot." In a post assassination *Life Magazine* interview, Jacqueline Kennedy confided to Theodore H. White, her late husband's partiality to the Broadway musical, and in particular, the closing lines of the title tune.

Not to be overshadowed, the Sorrel administration had its own residential relocation plan in place. My parents became part of the large-scale migration, also known as the White Exodus. During this affluent decade, minority groups seeking greater opportunity increasingly populated urban centers, while long-standing white residents began their diaspora departing for suburban and exurban areas.

Our red Super 88 Holiday Sports Sedan boasted great views, a 4-door sculpted body, downturned bumpers, and Fashion Flair diamond patterned interiors. All in all, proving true to the company's slogan, "There's something extra about owning an Oldsmobile!" This cherished conveyance saw us through peaks and valleys, so to speak—from refreshing summer joyrides to Bearskin Neck until a calamitous breakdown on The Fellsway, on a blazing hot day.

The middle child, stowed between older, Lorna, and kid sister, Diavola, I sat fidgeting as my flesh molded to the sticky upholstery, trying futilely not to make a jumble of my father's meticulous packing. My methodical dad had painstakingly assembled screws, bolts, and odds and ends in wooden cream cheese boxes and empty Mason jars. Minutes turned to hours as thirst, heat, and exhaustion sapped us while awaiting a tow truck. I had never before seen my father as defeated as he was on that sweltering afternoon. "Ah, fa Gawd's sake!" Sydney capitulated.

Our destination, Belmont, could be compared with a castle vintage or a *Château D'Yquem* for its rich, dry, white notes. The indigenous Pequosette inhabited this region, prior to the arrival of the first European settler, Roger Wellington, in 1636. The eponymous Wellington Hill, as it was known in the 19th century, consisted of little more than verdant fields, orchards, Strawberry Festivals, dairy farms, and pastures.

"Geography is Destiny," was Napoleon's official justification for imperialism. My family appropriated this statesmanship for our own expansionist plan to resettle to the 'burbs, to an epitome of safety and quietude, and the assurance of a better life. In his book, *A Murder in Belmont,* native son, Sebastian Junger, described, "There were no bars or liquor stores in Belmont. There were no homeless people in Belmont. There were no dangerous parts of Belmont, or poor parts of Belmont, or even ugly parts of Belmont."

Junger examines an unprecedented death that rocked this somnolent town. Sixty-three-year-old Bessie Goldberg was slain at her residence on Scott Road on March 11, 1963. Her killing occurred during the notorious 18-month reign of the Boston Strangler, or silk stocking murders, when thirteen women were sexually assaulted and then executed. Once unwary locals suddenly found themselves edgy. By eerie coincidence, the actual, self-confessed strangler, Albert DeSalvo, did handiwork at the Jungers' on the very day of this homicide.

Two miles from the crime scene, we ascended a hilltop to achieve our own version of the American Dream, arriving at Country Club Lane. Our new abode probably appeared to most passersby as little more than an ordinary split-level ranch house on a nondescript cul-de-sac abutting a sandlot. With a bottling plant and a golf course for neighbors, we still felt we had made it! The local fry criss-crossed this unfrequented dead end and its environs.

The Hill had its professional ruling class, its acreage, its gentility as well as its residing asylum. Harvard-affiliated McLean Hospital was always top tier. The incongruity of being a mere mile from Mill Street and *America's best freestanding psychiatric hospital,* (*US News and World Report*) was never lost on me, in spite of all the productive years squandered. How much better my life would have been if we had made that crucial detour during childhood. "It's the help you needed all along, but there was a lot going on," my father grudgingly conceded.

My schizoid personality disorder would go undiagnosed until my tumultuous 33rd year. Sadly most SPD's never are. That mystifying glitch accounts for why this covert state of affairs is fiercely more personally detrimental. The afflicted don't recognize their "adaptation" (Elinor Greenberg) and are not deleterious enough to others to warrant immediate concern.

On any given eve, Hill riders prowled a boundless swath, steering their bikes in figure eights and then orbiting the nearby rotary in tandem. Some plucky urchins lobbed kickballs willy-nilly onto carefully attended front yards. Those even more devil-may-care guttersnipes transgressed the extensive commercial properties at their own risk of trespassing.

Daylight hours merged with twilight, and my father began to bemoan the quotidian ritual of remanding me for the evening. Sitting down or still was not in my DNA, and neither apparently, was cracking the books. Sometimes he would resort to veiled ultimatums of getting the strap but knowing his passive disposition, I didn't feel the slightest bit remiss and kept right on playing without any regard for the hour or school the next day. Tumbling into bed wasn't a prelude to REM sleep, either.

My all-nighters deviated from those that class grinds pulled to secure straight A's. Bedwetting supplanted cramming. I experienced what I thought were stomach cramps in the wee hours, but they were likely psychosomatic. Sleep deprivation, admixed with panic from under preparation, had become cyclic. Mornings commenced as a rude awakening with my mother remonstrating, "Do your sleeping at night!" or "You were born tired!"—her alternating rejoinders to my usual resistance to rousing. (For most of my life, Henry Miller's *Insomnia: or, the Devil at Large* bedeviled me, but I later comprehended that it was depression and anxiety-related.)

Still groggy, I balked at the inevitable teasing I would provoke that day. Nonetheless, I made it out the door in a typically casual, literally half-assed departure. Racing for the bus, feeling a draft, realizing that I had stepped out of the homestead with a conspicuous hole in the crotch of my bloomers. Wardrobe malfunctions and fashion don'ts would be my cachet ever after.

Throughout my tutelage at Winn Brook School, the Principal, Mr. Blaney, registered as little more than a self-effacing, bespectacled, bald pate meandering through the corridors, overseeing the cafeteria staff in the lunchroom, or making an occasional, awkward suit-clad appearance near the dust filled sandbox. Like many administrators, he possessed a bland, featureless face and insipid deportment. He drew scant attention as he made his perfunctory rounds of the brick building with its low-slung water fountains, miniature furnishings, and Rorschach-like primary colors splattered in arresting, juvenile artwork.

Though Mr. Blaney did not make much of an impression on me, I must have made one on him or one of his underlings. And a highly aberrant one, even at a pudgy cheeked age of six. For the next thing I knew, my mother and aunt were escorting me to a barren room for something grownups called Miller Psychological Testing.

Mr. Miller's classroom contrasted with all others I had entered. I waited for the other little shavers to file in, but none arrived. A man sat me at a desk with a No. 2 pencil and a partially blank booklet freighted with lots of numbered words and pictures.

If this game were meant to replace my Saturday cartoons, I wasn't having nearly as much fun with it. Also, I couldn't grasp how this black and white edition would improve my speed like the *Evelyn Wood Reading Dynamics* advertised on TV.

No Mr. Miller or dunce cap in sight, to my enormous relief. Whatever happened with teachers, and me, and sometimes detention, my mother's homeschooling would amend. Liberated, I could pursue my own more naturalistic curriculum.

My parents likely resigned themselves to my lost cause status at this stage. Such distraction, lack of discipline, and panic attacks all rolled into one enervating loser. These stalwarts of The Greatest Generation promptly ceded to the woeful admission of having spawned a *Born Under A Bad Sign* under(Sheep)dog. Mother, never at a loss for words, formulated a newfound dismissive, "Just suited for manual labor." As if that axiom could be rubber-stamped on my wrist. This latest swipe, in effect, hand-canceled my self-assurance for a good many years.

Some teachers groused that I was staring out the window, not at the blackboard, much in the manner of a jailbird contemplating making a break. And with summer approaching, I would, indeed, be sprung, free to pursue my feral escapades. Spying an occasional pheasant in the brush or glimpsing an actual hobo with a stick bag traipsing to Route 2 were more enriching studies, as far as I was concerned. I was living on my own terms, my days akin to those of picaresque heroes or lovable rogues. Reveling in the physical world and revealing then and now, a far greater rapport with nonjudgmental critters.

My 4.7-mile fiefdom was one in the same with a treasure hunt. The workaday world, conversely, was my parents'

Astroturf, or indoors, their carpeted one. Outside versus inside polarities. "Me versus them" sensibilities. And even indoors versus indoors divides—my mother confined to her office, a cubicle in a converted mudroom, while pater familias tarried for long hours at the office. They were truly more married to the business than to each other. Both emanated from the rank and file and surmounted the storied penury of The Great Depression, so I fully accepted their striving for solvency. Especially with kiddos and a mortgage to support.

Sometimes we ventured out as a family, but sporadically. Our trip to the Franklin Park Zoo was only noteworthy because upon sighting a massive beast with gargantuan protuberances on its skull, an elk, I inquired of my parents, "What's that?" "It's a horn," my dad responded succinctly. "Well, don't let him blow it at me," was my artless reply.

At or around the time the Berlin Wall was constructed (August 13, 1961), the distaff side of the family, namely, my mother, leveled her own defense against the distaff side of my father's family, notably, his mother.

My father, ne Sorocovitch, had Mother Russia as his very own. *Heimisch* with a highly inflected voice and down-to-earth, dry goods bearing, Blanche had the unmitigated temerity to attend my parents' nuptials in a shabby dress. For this misdeed, there would be no reprieve.

Further, this grande dame never acknowledged her only son, Sydney's, birthday. "After you've been in labor for so many hours, you never forget," Gertrude reminded us. Whereupon we would never be allowed to forget the pain of our deliveries and the additional pangs her mother-in-law induced.

What's more, my mother installed her own chimeric redoubt buttressing us from my father's family to the maximum extent. Henceforth, they may not visit us, but we could see them when she was involved in day-to-day business operations.

Besides the almighty buck, my parents basically bonded over their mutual contempt for the prefabricated McMansions of nearby Hillcrest. Those brash arrivistes in their garish, cookie-cutter blots on the landscape drew snickers and other expressions of overt disdain. In some respects, their professional ties and leisure activities seemed as parvenu to me. But what they most appeared to be was increasingly blindsided, their almost exclusive emphasis on my father's prosperity foremost to any immediate or palpable concerns for their progeny's welfare.

What she may have lacked in maternal instincts, my mother possessed in savvy as she could sniff the winds of post-war change. With fast foods and convenience products on the uptick, she recognized that the country was transitioning from a manufacturing to a service economy.

Behind every successful man, there is a strong woman, and Gertrude was no exception. Her vision was 20/20 when it came to overhauling Sydney's practice into a newfangled mecca. Her brainchild allowed patients to order glasses immediately after an eye exam. Somerset Optical premiered. The arrival of one-stop shopping proved popular and lucrative.

Fresh, more urbane surroundings meant more sophisticated playmates and pranks. My father worked progressively longer hours and seemed more preoccupied and susceptible.

"Hi, Daddy, what do you call a sprained knee in medical terminology?" I inquired mincingly.

"A subluxation of the semilunar cartilage, why?" he replied without looking up from his Leica 35 mm.

"Oh, nothing. One of my friends...," I pressed.

My dad was probably relieved I had a social life and gave it little thought.

"Would you mind writing that on a slip of paper so I don't forget?" I insisted.

"Okay. Here," he assented.

"Could you sign it so it's more authentic?" I persisted.

"Um, sure," he scribbled his indecipherable John Hancock and handed it back to me mechanically so he could check the lens mount.

"Thank you." Our repartee concluded, and my "pal" was exempted from gym class over the next few days.

Such bartering of services on the open cafeteria market often resulted in upsell sandwich trades, and any delicacies laden with mayonnaise made the bidding escalate. To my medical parents, this condiment was a deplorable semi-solid fat.

Our lane encompassed a disparate coterie that readily became friends. My mother associated with a bookish *Sudeten* couple whose home was adorned with handcrafted, white birch limb lamps, shelves, and other furnishings formerly from the trees of their own backyard. During winters, residents shook the snowfall from these wispy charmers to preclude breakage. Delicate, darker birches also abounded. Gray Birch Circle flanked our lane and looked like an overgrown knoll where perchance, trolls, or other woodland creatures, might dwell.

After school, I stopped at the Czech household to aid with dinner while the grizzled wife was recovering from a skiing accident. Crossing their threshold I traveled back in time. I entered the bijou, putatively yesteryear warmth and ostensible charm of a quaint, *Those Were the Days* home. The air was aromatized from Central European style simmering broths heaped with vegetables that also came from their garden. Their lifestyle was the closest approximation of farm-to-table back then.

The wife's leg lingered in a cast for at least six weeks, which at the time seemed like an eternity. The husband was also homebound with some kind of illness, but he appeared the same as he always had, except he wasn't outdoors shaking trees or indoors crafting furniture. My parents were reticent about his mental problems, never elaborating on what that meant. I ministered to the wife by repositioning her shank for greater ease. I didn't know what I was supposed to do for the husband, except perhaps massage his head?

We upheld a Country Club Lane code of silence. Another tight-lipped one was the rabbi down the street. Although a *macher* (Yiddish for big cheese), he usually donned the same outfit. I wondered why this man of high standing almost invariably wore a lady's black gown? If he couldn't afford a more extensive wardrobe, how could he live on The Hill? My mother didn't have any answers to my sartorial inquiries but advised me to slow down when biking past his house, along with, of course, not breaking any Commandments or doing anything unruly in his presence.

Sloan Wilson's *The Man in the Gray Flannel Suit* was a mid-fifties parable of corporate conformity. Although my father headed his own enterprise, he hewed to such conservative garb. My initial impression of his stocky, ashen, and hairless conformation sheathed in this neutral color recalled a baby elephant, and so it became known as his elephant suit. Pachyderm Papa, dapper Babar's American son. Unlike the nearby cleric, our breadwinner owned other polyester Sears and Roebuck ensembles, often hyping their price points and packability.

One eye-catching hottie predated social x-rays when Tom Wolfe minted the term in 1987 in *Bonfire of the Vanities*. Gym trim with long black hair, she was often seen in the open in the same attire, a skimpy two-piece bathing suit, as she went about her yard work during warmer weather. I pondered whether she wore swimwear or less inside? Surrounding *domestic engineers* who were considerably more robust tssked in disapproval, but if "genetic Lotto" existed, she won, and I lauded her individualism. Living across the street, she eyed our protracted landscaping efforts and gave a copy of Hazel Perper's *The Avocado Pit Grower's Indoor How-to-Book* to mom. I never understood then or now how an entire publication could be written on this self-evident horticultural topic. Aside from my mother's redoing (or, in the opinion of some others, denuding) our front yard to plant flowering trees and other shrubberies for greater privacy, we were the only house to have a sunken garden in its living room with immense *Monstera* leaves, a pebble footway, and a Japanese stone garden lantern.

Maria, a contemporary and a potential acquaintance, resided a few doors away. My mother mentioned she was a princess, although she lacked a tiara or exceptional pulchritude. She did, however, seem to rule her Italian-American parents. Her mother applauded me for kindling in her *ragazza* an *apetito* for tomato-based dishes. Curiously, this should have seemed like second nature to someone of this culture. The father liked that I was easy to please. His Daddy Gimme daughter was definitely much higher maintenance than I and ridiculed my handbag selection, from the safe vantage of her bedroom window. Popping her head out of the casement, as would a Jackie in the Box, she hurled one salvo after another when I passed their house. Her major grievance involved my wearing an out of season accessory.

My first pocketbook marked an eventual rite of passage to *Seventeen Magazine* and Tussy's Enchanté Cologne. Gertrude probably nabbed whatever girl's purse was available at a thrift store, and I was much too ingenuous to grasp that floral connoted primaveral. This diva hectored me for depending on it year-round. Her folks, who probably wished they had a kiddie who was content with just one of any item, encouraged my on and off, basic budget presence.

Variants of occupational deprivation adages prosper. In *The Proverbs of John Heywood*, written in 1546, he discerns,

"'But who is wurs shod, than the shoemaker's wyfe, with shops full of newe shapen shoes all her lyfe," or as the more familiar trope, "the cobbler's children have no shoes," "a plumber's house always has a dripping tap," and "a blacksmith's home only has wooden spoons."

None exist for the anomaly of the ophthalmologist's daughter flunking a grade school eye test. *Jeepers Creepers!* But that's exactly how I acquired an integral accessory, the one I wore ceaselessly, all year round, days and nights, until I could no longer read the minuscule letters on the last line of the optician's chart or even some of the others above. Although glasses did improve my vision markedly, my focus remained far from laser-like. Mother had occasional parent-teacher meetings but seemed more attuned to child sociology than psychology. She regaled my father at dinner with tales of the flatulence that caused Miss Greener to implore, "Children, children, please...."

The era known as The Atomic Age was punctuated by mandatory air raid responsiveness training. Duck and cover practice was as prevalent as today's fire drills. The Soviet Union's threat of a nuclear blast left families on the alert. Studying at home handbooks stoked fears or abetted preparation, depending upon your point of view. On the spur of the moment, a siren sounded, and we then found ourselves caching under our school desks, or at the very least, covering or concealing our heads. President Kennedy advocated for the building of fallout shelters, digging holes in our backyards, and stocking them with life's necessities to survive this imminent disaster. Think of it as a ginormous go bag in the ground.

The newly constructed Fresh Pond Shopping Center steadily became my minder. En route to my father's office during a weekend day, my parents would deposit my sisters and me at this strip mall for extended periods, almost as a regular would drop off the weekly dry cleaning load. We would rove from store to store and mostly window shop on our meager allowances. Five-and-dime emporium, F.W. Woolworth, Zayre, and the Fresh Pond Cinema were our preferred hangouts, as our threesome were precursors to latter-day mall rats.

We certainly qualified as very mall-adjusted without realizing it. Woolworth's Luncheonettes had specials for kids to pop a balloon for a chance to get a free banana split. Zayre had unmatched selections of discounted merchandise and was our go-to for back-to-school shopping. Seeing some movies several times or venturing between screening rooms became habitual pastimes. When our mother enlisted our help in stickering prices on frames for the optical shop, we began to recognize some of the styles on the sought after actors. Oscar nominee George C. Scott sported the best-selling "Dainty Rounds" in *Patton*.

While films provided a respite from school doldrums, the office, and my parents' spasmodic strife, I read voraciously, devouring a period piece children's book series conveying traditions and domestic stability among five varied sisters on the Lower East Side of New York in 1912. Sydney Taylor's *All-of-a-Kind Family* series was a hospitable snuggery, and all I could have wished for as an idealized home life.

The Cold War effects dawdled, and the world as we knew it was profoundly shaken one fall morning. All families and nations reeled to learn of the assassination of John Fitzgerald Kennedy in Dallas, Texas, on November 22, 1963. This devastating milestone was probably the most pivotal rupture of the century. The shooting was on Gertrude's birthday—all we could muster that day and for more to come, were tears. My first deep-rooted episode of mourning at eight was for someone we all felt we knew and liked but had never even met.

The pall of this favored president's passing shrouded the

holidays but still permitted my parents to board the SS France for an overdue luxury vacation. We daughters were shuttled to either a maternal sister or brother, which meant staying in Brooklyn or Bayside, respectively. At variance were both places from each other and our town! My mother often touched on prized childhood vignettes of her Flatbush rearing, but she had only vituperative language for East New York.

"There's a saying in Brownsville that says that if you're 25, you're either dead, or in jail, or you're done with the gang life," photographer Reed Young remarked. "Get out of Brooklyn," Gertrude beseeched her elder sister and brother-in-law during the tempestuous '60's. They never did, but now Breukelen, or Broken Land to the Dutch settlers of the 1600's, bolsters 700 arts and cultural attractions.

Avenue N. in Midwood, deep in the Borough of Kings, was my actual landing place that December. I stayed alone with my unobtrusive accountant uncle, Seymour, his more flamboyant bookkeeper wife, Millie, and a somewhat younger male cousin, Larry, in their monochrome apartment. The novelty of iridescent tropical fish cavorting in their recessed wall tank fascinated me throughout the entire sojourn.

Christmas dictated Chinese food takeout, and then so did New Year's Eve. My relatives tried to make me feel more at home by allowing me to help feed the fish. My affable uncle seemed to appreciate my interest, indicating the different breeds and their habits. As a special treat, he let me listen to some of his cosseted, boxed vinyl Judy Garland sets. "Isn't she beautiful?" he glowed while gingerly extracting fan photos from her estimable performance at Carnegie Hall in 1961 and stared lovingly at them. Through the bay window, the winter street scenery became encrusted with swirling flurries enrobing the bulky cars, ornamental windmill, and compact hedges. This nostalgic vista rekindled shaking a snow globe with the uplifting homeyness of being inside.

We were truly related, but so very dissimilar. My aunt never appropriated her younger sister's frequent lamentation that she was "surrounded by idiots" even when she was clearly miffed. My uncle genuinely seemed to care about me besides running errands together. My cousin, as an only child, was showered with the kind of doting that neither my siblings nor I ever savored.

Chapter 3

Of Tiny Racks
and Rear Attacks

Race relations were on the tip of everyone's tongue in 1964. President Johnson signed into law the landmark Civil Rights Act, ensuring that Negroes and other minorities could no longer be denied service based on the color of their skin. We Americans were now one people. My biology teacher, Mrs. Hickey, offered her own proof of our unanimity as a correlation to this breakthrough legislation. A little-known fact, she confided to my class in a low-pitched confessional tone, is that Negroes, or "colored" babies as they were then designated, are born Caucasian and darken postpartum giving them that telltale pigmentation. I casually alluded to this state-of-the-art Darwinism when I returned home that afternoon. My parents decried this quackery over dinner, even proposing my removal from school. Mrs. Hickey's sotto voce, pseudo-science may have proved fortuitous.

Assisting my mother in the garden was truly a labor of love. Captivating hummingbirds often fluttered at the azalea flowers. Incandescent fireflies sparked the air with their magic. Sometimes at sundown, when my mother and I were watering the front yard, a russet-haired Scandinavian sidled up to gossip. Gertrude gave her the once-over, complimenting her new beehive. Hearing that, I kept my distance so as not to get stung. I soon discovered that her tongue was even more acerbic as she habitually referred to me, my sisters, and even her own brood as "the stupes." My mother threw us under the school bus.

Rock and roll had yet to ripple to our shoreline. Cultured girls and boys learned social grace in ballroom dancing classes at Winn Brook. As the instructor matched me with the next available partner, my hands became clammy, my voice muffled, and my posture tauter. My Fred Astaire epiphany on the threshold of adolescence was that intimacy, no matter how innocuous or even public, was antipathetic to me. The instructor and partner also acknowledged my gross discomfiture but were too tactful to call attention to it. The lessons recurred, remaining a forbidding weekly tween ritual.

Pleasure trips were another matter entirely, and I was thrilled to travel with my class, especially with the prospect of an upcoming excursion to the United Nations. We would make the journey all in one day, including a stopover for supper at Valle's Steak House for a meat and greet. I was gobsmacked that the bus driver could accomplish this tour so efficiently as driving to my relatives required staying overnight. While we may have crossed state lines, this outing transformed my classmates and me into global citizens.

More junkets south to New York made the vistas feel familiar. My mother gabbed with Barney, her optical salesman acquaintance, who offered rides from The Bay State to The Empire State so she could visit her kin more often. These commercial passages were playing hooky providential. (Not to mention, a far greater quota of milk chocolate than was permissible at home.) Gertrude and Barney parlayed the latest spectacle styles as *Women's Wear Daily* might preview a Fashion Week. The passing tolls, monotonous shop talk, and candy's Theobromine lulled me into a caloric complacency.

Traversing the sinister Bronx with its monolithic Co-op City complex, I would have cowered at the possibility of getting lost (got that a lot) in such an anonymous-looking bastion. How do children find their way home when everything is identical? When we zipped by during the holidays, the appearance of Christmas lights blinkering the rear windows baffled me, as they were visible mostly to oblivious pigeons roosting on the fire escapes.

Daddy was even more disinterested, so I adopted two new fathers in 1964—talk show hosts, David Frost and Merv Griffin. They were far more adept at chit-chat than I and definitely much more gregarious. And the best part about it, I could turn them on or off at will. Sometimes I assimilated too verbatim what their guests offered by way of guidance. One hip therapist vilified the lack of honesty in our society, egging on the TV audience to be more candid. I took his advice to heart and to school the very next day.

An off guard teacher polled the assembled students as to whether they wished to know the provenance of, "Seek and ye shall find?" (It's Matthew 7:7.) The usual brown-nosers and fawning sycophants waved frenetically in full-bore hyperkinesis. Inexplicably, she pointed to me. A symbolic lightbulb illuminated. Now was my chance to mentor my class on what I had learned. Recalling precisely what that clinician recommended, I declined her explanation categorically. I was to employ psycho jargon, an authentic self, or my own person even then. No, I did not want to know!

The tube therapist may have won this round, but I lost it and found myself cast, once again, in the all too familiar role of a troublemaker (a.k.a. outstanding pupil). Aaron Neville's *Tell It Like It Is* ranked in Billboard's Top 100 a couple of years later, making this idiom hep.

With more disposable income, families hit the open road in droves. Our geography class embraced this "It's the journey, not the destination." Eyes riveted on a chalkboard woven with the country's latticework of highways. At the mention of a byway, I swiveled and waved behind me. Teacher's pet, stolid Eddie, full belly cackled, becoming uncharacteristically an outstanding pupil that day. *Bye Bye Birdie.*

If looks could kill, I'd be dead right now. (I have one foot in the grave from being schizoid for so long.) Appearances could sometimes rattle me, but I usually kept my commentary to myself. Assertive Jody possessed an irremovable African slave bracelet. My heart extended to that pitiable servant whose shackle had become this white chick's accessory a century after the Emancipation Proclamation. Whenever she approached, I averted my eyes, trying to forget this hateful vestige of the Antebellum South.

Sometimes student exchanges resulted in inadvertent disparagement. Jody remarked to another in my presence that I 'had a brain, but she doesn't use it.' Demeaning, yes, lack of insight into my handicap, without a doubt. Maybe her rangy self towering over meek me or her general smugness spiked my anxiety? Probably all of the above. How I wished to evaporate, but recoiled instead into my comfy, imaginary buffer. Jody's superiority tweaked the visceral reaction that gnawed at me during my mother's baseless rant, "I want Blair to be able to take care of herself!" Flummoxed as what child that age could, or, for that matter, should? "They strike at what they don't understand," a social worker offered years later. Hoping that adults were much kinder beings would show once and for all to be wishful thinking.

Wiseacres and I mixed like Filippo Berio and Évian-les-Bains. Audacious, with lips curled in a perpetual smirk, Dale's mere presence proved disconcerting. Highly opinionated and obstreperous, he sneered at me for being flat chested and other perceived figure flaws.

I tried deflecting Dale (Jody, Louisa, and other aggressors) by depressing the nozzle of my make-believe aerosol mace. It didn't work. As the Big Man on Campus prattled, my head spun, rendering my reply inchoate. "I can't believe how dumb you are," he plumed himself. Zoning out, I could not go tit for tat.

Body changes were beginning to affect relations and not necessarily sexually. Invasive Jody really hit below the belt one day. She summoned her retinue, motioning to my callipygian endowment. What the Greeks and Romans revered (All hail "Venus of the Beautiful Buttocks"), she reviled. The next century would permit JLo and Kim Kardashian to spearhead our movement, and life for the once defamed bottom heavy would eventually top out.

What worry through yonder window breaks? Little tykes develop motor skills drawing houses. Our teacher taught by rote with no real latitude. When I finished the frame, I fretted about the dormers, unable to suppress my *shpilkes*.

"Look, sister, I'll let you know when we'll start them," the churlish instructor snapped.

Were we related? More pins and needles than in a sewing kit and more piercing, spontaneous outpourings. Teachers fobbed off my impulsive one-line interjections with formulaic two-word rebuttals, "Cool it!," "big mouth," or "no Kleenex."

Dentophobia. My visits became a three-man job (four if

you count the dental tech.). My mother was my lady-in-waiting, in Dr. Bilitis' office and remained in the exam room itself, holding my hand during multiple abortive Novocain injection attempts. A wet nurse to my ocular floodgates opening and that freaking cavity finally closing.

Being so much in one's own little world causes unfortunate collateral damage. On the rare occasion of my father having an afternoon off during the summer, we made a beeline to transcendentalist Walden Pond on a true scorcher. Casting pebbles and watching their momentary limpid undulations was intriguing. I was too impervious to the helplessness of other swimmers. When tossing rock crystals; one hit the shoulder of a young boy, and he flinched. Oops! I have never ever forgotten his ached expression or fully forgiven myself for my unwitting role in striking him.

Excessive self-absorption, the hallmark of schizoid personality disorder (SPD or SzPD), underscores such insensitivity and poor social judgment. Even in a classroom, I often forgot where I was. Termagants rebuked my rubber band slingshots, humming, doing everything short of masturbating in default mode. "This is not a beauty parlor," Neo-Darwinist, Mrs. Hickey, reproached me for brushing my tresses. This is not a biology class, either, I mused.

Ten ushered in men. During this turning point of a year, 1965, I developed my first ever crush on a somewhat older fella, a snappy dresser with classic good looks and an enviable sense of adventure. Jonny Quest. We shared the same recalcitrance to formal education, and I marveled at his exploits and entourage (adopted Hadji and dog, Bandit). Mostly, I longed for a parent who, like his scientist and phenomenologist dad, Dr. Benton C. Quest, functioned as my best friend and included me in all the action.

The Quests were exceptional explorers, but average Americans were traveling more those days, so accommodating fast food and restaurant chains began to proliferate.

Nearby IHOP and Howard Johnson's emerged as student hangouts as did local pizzerias. The sixties saw a meteoric rise in demand for this Italian import.

Pizza adjoins Christopher Columbus, confirming that the world is not only round but flat. While a slice may not upstage Proust's madeleine or be as American as apple pie, this gooey masterpiece holds an endearing place in most people's hearts.

A paean to an atypical pie, this delicacy rightfully supplanted the standard rubber chicken entrée at functions. A snack or a meal, you decide, that's more democratic in spirit since everyone can afford it. A memory maker as everybody has a venue, topping, and association. A bit player from some of my generation's favorite flicks (*Saturday Night Fever, Manhattan*) with its own red carpet appearance at the Oscars one year. A thinker outside the box before becoming a bromide.

Pizza was our mainstay on Sunday nights, a savory departure from the usual lackluster repast. An eat and run affair forfending the need to idle at the table in this uneasy household. The only volatility it evoked was the time Diavola reheated the mouthwatering Belmont Pizza, lodging it carton and all, into the oven. "Would you put a newspaper in there?" my father yelped when flames shot up.

Another slice of life was visiting classmate Betty on Leonard Street in vibrant Belmont Center. A ringside seat to her mother and sisters' scrambling to prepare simple meals with pots clanging amid a cramped kitchen suggested true home-lovingness. Everyone did what was needed, and nobody seemed to mind the pantry congestion or chores. Her amiable mother recounted her own salad days' follies as we were prepubescents in the throes of our own.

Heading onto Clifton Street on the return trek, I longed for Dr. Quest and Mrs. Mahoney as surrogate parents as we would set out on exciting escapades far beyond any dreary Greater

Boston hearth. Not that I didn't feel any closeness with mine but "Gomez" was as detached as "Morticia" was domineering. The ambiguity of not feeling treasured would taint my trust in others and rankle my self-esteem for some time.

Maybe they wanted a boy? An entire month after my birth, I remained Jane Doe, Junior. Judeo-Christianity allots a week or so for naming ceremonies; Hinduism stages *Namkaran* belatedly on the neonate's eleventh or twelfth day. Cousin Itt, meet your distant flesh and blood, Miss Whatchamacallit, of our own *Addams Family*, the white sheep.

Perhaps, as with Mrs. Hickey's theory, they hoped, once oxidized, I would transgender. In any event, they were stuck with this make, like it or not.

What's in a name? Shakespeare trivialized its import, but I was saddled with an androgynous, exotic one for the era.

Blair bore repetition so often as to become a bugbear.

Often I went by my alter ego, Claire, having long wearied of the nomenclature clarifications. That's close enough; I thought when called.

With the advent of broadcasting, worlds beyond nuclear families enlarged. Televisions were affordable and common, so many now became dining room fixtures. Marshall McLuhan's canon, "The medium is the message," was spot on as the viewing audience grew vaster. The imminent arrival of four Liverpudlians would confirm this catchline and alter our prior cultural and musical sensibilities perpetually.

In his work, *Revolution in the Head: The Beatles Records and the Sixties*, Ian MacDonald labels The Fab Four as "perfect McLuhanites," "who felt their way through life." Their zingy ad-libs and facetious press conferences distinguished them from prior vapid, homogenized groups. A staggering 73 million viewers, a record number, tuned into The Beatles' debut on the *Ed Sullivan Show* on February 9, 1964. Not a single NYC juvenile crime was reported during this telecast.

Beatlemania was unleashed. This avant-garde quartet that brought such unprecedented color and verve to the world sang five standards (*She Loves You, All My Loving, Till There Was You, I Saw Her Standing There, and I Want to Hold Your Hand*) to an exclusively black and white television audience.

Multitudes of females were smitten with "the cute Beatle," Paul. Both sexes admired their longer 'dos so much so that they became a collectable, The Mop Top wig.

Even so, their attitude was their most compelling attribute; as Hanif Kureshi considered, "The Beatles became heroes to the young because they were not deferential: no authority had broken their spirit; they were confident and funny; they answered back; no one put them down."

A schizoid connoisseur could only fantasize about harboring these characteristics. My classmate, Julia, dreamed, as did legions of worshipful girls, women, and likely some men, of possessing Paul all to herself. "Well, how long did you expect him to wait for you?" her mother reflected wryly when the most in demand Beatle finally wed Linda Eastman.

Brainy, blond Russian spy, Ilya Kuryakin (British actor, David McCallum) of *The Man from U.N.C.L.E.* stole other impressionable hearts. *The World of Henry Orient* with Peter Sellers showcased a teenage girl's infatuation and single-minded pursuit of a wacky concert pianist. Most adolescents will transition to flesh and blood love objects over time. Circumspect schizoids may never, no matter their age. The higher functioning among my constituency might marry and even have children, but remain guarded.

The theme of the 1964 New York World's Fair was "Peace through Understanding." If only this slogan could have pacified the fractious crush reactive to the heat index and hidden costs. Arriving at Flushing Meadows on a teeming city bus during the dog days, the humidity intensified. Sitting wedged in a packed car beneath a panoply of scented, glistening armpits, I experienced a pungent contact high. Still, I would have gladly traded this wonder whiff for a cold soda quaffed on my only in a shady spot in the backyard.

The Fair's 650 acres offered many options and much wrangling. Finally, we went with the popular choice; the scrumptious Belgian waffle stand in its Tudor shack. The clever Vermersch proprietors capitalized on the American sweet tooth. By adding a dollop of schlag and fresh cut strawberries to the standard Brussels' fare, they drew at times an astounding 2500 customers a day. The raw ingredients sizzling in a 500-degree cast iron pan produced a celestially light 99-cent chef d'oeuvre. A star was born even if the Fair was a bust.

By mid-decade, The Great Society superseded *Camelot*, Jackie rebounded as a placid widow, and rumblings of a potential conflict in Asia became more audible. Both of my parents were Second World War and Korea veterans; my father attended medical school on the G.I. Bill (The Servicemen's Readjustment Act of 1944). Their service and patriotism were occasionally at odds with left-leaning Belmont. To some in this upscale town, Sorrel women would come to epitomize odd men out.

Material comfort paved the way for more mingling. The nuclear family would never qualify as big social mixers. The Hospitality Committee did not greet their usually impromptu guests with canapés on a sterling platter or any dish resembling a *Good Housekeeping* recipe rave. An *Addams Family* evening would not suggest revelry to the clinking of cocktail glasses or other indications of suburban debauchery. The Hill elitists seeking such conviviality should instead join the country club next door.

The backyard rock garden was becoming a source of civic pride. Mother and I spent a sultry, arduous weekend afternoon weeding and planting phlox among the rocky ledges. After several strenuous hours, mud embedded my nails and caked my clothes. Resolved to freshening up, I retired to the bathroom. While showering, Gertrude's hen party clustered, jabbering beyond the door. "Is she also budding?" one of her cringeworthy girlfriends stage whispered.

Whenever possible, I gave the slip to them. Now, these dames wrested their revenge, and I was held hostage in the toilet of my own home, reduced to a one-person nudist colony. Naked, going nowhere slowly.

Immured with two mute companions, department store statues Venus de Milo and David, I waited for these unwelcome guests to vamoose. They did at last, so I could emerge from my private Plato's Retreat clad in a chic ensemble of pink hand and bath towels. "It's like having another cat in the house," mother declared of my glaringly secretive nature.

Rowdy sorts made me all the stealthier. My parents remained sanguine that fraternizing with other children would coax me to come out of my shell. The more may have been the merrier for most. A packed house prompted me to take a powder. But never let it be said that I hid under the bed.

Gertrude and Sydney's best friends also had three daughters. We saw these counterparts in school, Lieb's Deli, our place of worship, and when we joined forces with them on local excursions. If we gathered for variety and value, then Chinese was palate-pleasing grub.

Cantonese was the only regional cuisine at that time. Venues were often festooned with lots of red and gold geegaws, the preeminent "dragons and lanterns school of design" while serving lobster sauce loaded dishes. We were seated and in a few short minutes, Dad's buddy, Earl, metamorphosized into the kind of customer servers universally detest. You probably know the type. Flying a freak flag over free Jasmine tea. "Don't keep using that same bag!" he lambasted the obsequious waiter scurrying and sloshing in servitude. My stomach roiled throughout this whole parsimonious display, and the drive home made me even more bilious. I don't recall what I sampled that day or what anyone discussed, but how desolate I felt and my firm wish that we would never again meet for a fun run.

Country Club Lane Culture Vultures circled as we made our Temple rounds. At nine, I could whine or request in the words of sportswriter Ring Lardner to "include me out." Mother became more active in her Sisterhood with its president effusing about her evident flair in decorating an event's dining hall fussing, "Gert Sorrel's masterful hands," in an adulatory blurb in their newsletter. She couldn't stomach seeing her sobriquet in print, but basked in the accolade.

Four commendatory words in that publication. My mother was gifted for all to see, and in spite of our conflicted rapport, I felt honored for her. Her paperwork was laborious but unfulfilling. We probably would have been a tighter-knit family had she been more content.

My mother had panache. One of her clique complimented her home decor, remarking to the other women, "See, this is what you can do when you have money." In all candor, my parents were impecunious during those early years. Among her many talents, Gertrude had gumption (another trait that I inherited) and could create the illusion of more substance.

During my father's medical residency in St. Louis, and when longing for a hometown pizza, they prepared their own, even if it meant settling for ersatz American cheese. They both tended to an orphaned rabbit housed in a cleansed, mid-century vintage ashtray stand—and which Daddy fed with an eye dropper. Mommy was enthusiastic about the variegated coleus growing copiously outside. Their animated accounts reinforced that despite their privations, childless, they were more harmonious.

"Like sugar, pure sugar!" Gertrude extolled, munching on

a watermelon slab. "Water-meeh-loon!" she and her brother, George, would roar, imitating Italian immigrants' heavily accented mispronunciation of this luscious Victory garden gourd. In their prime, they behaved as a complicit comedy team, reenacting the same schtick.

Suddenly her flashback fizzled. Sydney breached her La-la-land. A cumbersome dining stool dwarfed his elfin build. In her eyes, my Mister Rogers-like father morphed into a Neanderthal, dragging not a chair but a cavewoman by her scalp.

"Look, it can absorb any weight and not leave impressions," he began to effervesce. Taking its frame forthrightly, he rammed it spasmodically into the newly installed linoleum. The legs jackhammered the arabesque pattern as he pounded furiously. With each drubbing, Gertrude began squawking, growing more keyed up with every thrust. "You're drunk!" she railed. So much for "a beautiful day" in the neighborhood. (*Won't You Be My Neighbor?*)

Her grandmother had goaded her to become a doctor. The war disrupted everyone's lives, and many ambitions went unrealized. Gertrude sought achievement through my father and vicariously through her daughters for what had been her atrophied past. Be that as it may, she was becoming a pillar of Belmontian society.

Attendees at a recent bar mitzvah were dumbfounded when they got to the buffet. The edible centerpiece was none other than the likeness of the son of the commandment molded into a concoction of chicken liver, schmaltz, onions, and hard-cooked eggs. A 27-second look-see of this near-perfect mimesis and mere minutes before gourmandize demolished this "What am I, chopped liver?" work, Gertrude found her new calling.

Soon thereafter, she began sculpting busts but in more enduring pumice. These rough-hewn pieces evinced a striking resemblance to truncated versions of Easter Island primitives. One clay modeling resurrected the features of the attractive 35th president. She was truly dexterous, demonstrating her *sui generis* knack for splitting apples. Gertrude's masterful hands seemed made to manipulate or thump their material, be it pumice, clay, or my own fragile psyche.

Chapter 4

The Upside of a Dark Side

David Lean's epic *Dr. Zhivago* was shot mostly in torrid Spain, yet achieved some of film history's most bone-chilling scenes of Bolshevik Russia. Fresh Pond's superfluous air conditioning contributed to the *cinema verité* numbing its shivering audience during the ongoing, lengthy snowscapes. While commiserating with Omar Sharif's/Yuri's bloodshot eyes and frozen mustache as he teetered en route to Yuriatin searching for his Lara, hairs bristled on my goosebumped arms. After over three hours, I, too, lost sensation in my extremities in this torture chamber of a screening room. As much as I fancied the forbidden romance, breathtaking scenery, and sumptuous sets, my sister and I, in a nearly vacant matinee, couldn't generate enough combined body heat to offset the polar cap. Why didn't mom make us bring sweaters? Welcome to the cold and cruel world.

On another occasion, Diavola chuckled uncontrollably and gesticulated so broadly at the slapstick, that she knocked her glasses off her face, and they landed several rows away. In the dark, we couldn't fumble on the viscid floor looking for them and likely disturbing the other patrons, so she shared my pair, our moiety-focals. We would view the comedy again to take in the other half.

Leaving us for so many youthful hours at the picture show, my sister and I soon became acquainted with a very galvanizing loner.

Needs no introduction, "The Man with No Name," but he also went by "Joe," "Manco," and "Blondie." He is the poncho-clad Clint Eastwood title role of Sergio Leone's popular spaghetti western trilogy, an anti-hero of the first order, and a possible member of my very own and little understood, good, bad, and sometimes ugly kinsfolk. *A Fistful of Dollars* rolled out, and so did a different kind of starring role. I saw a compatriot on the silver screen and a true hero to those of us that, for better or worse, go it alone. One with his own moral compass, who may ultimately prove ethical but does not achieve the desired outcome through convention. Although any blood sport or violence is abhorrent to me, watching this laconic bounty hunter vanquish insuperable obstacles in his understated, singular way was mesmerizing. Scraggly, terse, and manifestly his own person, "No Name" had a divergent claim to fame.

Another recluse gained a high profile, *Nowhere Man.* This hermit emanated from the wondrous fountainhead of John Lennon, who admitted in interviews that "the song is probably about myself." Lennon toiled with song writer's block for five cantankerous hours until this anthem wrote itself. This somber piece marked a sea change from the lighthearted titles of the Lennon and McCartney collaboration and a foreshadowing of the deeper, more inscrutable themes their partnership would explore.

Tunes centered on the marginalized as more acknowledged, if not generally accepted, were becoming faddish. Most emblematic of this trend was The Doors' release of *People Are Strange* (1967.) "It's music for the different, the uninvited," narrates Johnny Depp, in American Masters/Tom DiCillo's *When You're Strange: A Film About The Doors*, 2010. Jim Morrison "wrote from the position of being a lonely, alienated person... Jim had a darkness in his writing...in his life," commented biographer James Riordan, in *Break on Through: The Life and Death of Jim Morrison* ("Jim Morrison: The Final 24" documentary).

Melancholic babies commingled with melodramatic ladies in Maine in a campy Gothic-style soap opera, *Dark Shadows*. No other daytime serial could claim a vampire in its cast, but Barnabas Collins got all the attention. We both required orthodonture, brooked uncommon names, and desported ourselves as restless creatures of the night. Finding no ally in my immediate surroundings, I sought landsmen wherever I could locate them. Other kids also felt the enticement of this series and raced recklessly to sit transfixed in front of Collinwood Mansion. "...we received several letters and phone calls saying that children were disregarding safety measures in their haste to get home after school for the program," San Antonio's Channel 12 KSAT cautioned. Fortunately, I lived to see the light of day, the next episode, and then some 1,224 more.

A somberly silhouetted society was apparent with dark *The Graduate* and black *Who's Afraid of Virginia Woolf?* Film comedies were limning the aesthetic horizon. Even minstrels Simon and Garfunkel plumbed a more pensive mood in their reverential ode to blind Columbian, Sanford Green in *The Sound of Silence*. Not all despairing, mind you. The Beach Boys'

Good Vibrations and The Turtles' *Happy Together* are indicative of the countervailing jubilant music consistent with a more carefree, fifties' carryover vibe.

For me, the period wasn't the all-popular smiley faces. Amid flower children, I blossomed into a mushroom child. And a penetrative grade school teacher, Miss Dygas, was alert enough to sense something amiss. At 11, I was a chip off the old *Addams Family* block. My *Paint it Black* bias, discernibly dour predisposition, and wild dog of Borneo-style guttural schoolroom grunts fazed her. She began to wonder about my domestication and encouraged starting a notebook of my more perverse, morose ruminations. (My only regret is that I didn't retain that binder.) Miss Dygas didn't see a red flag for the Massachusetts Department of Children or Families or the deranged cogitation of a latent homicidal maniac. What she perceived instead, pouting on the periphery of her classroom, was a perpetually sullen girl and a possible J.D., acronym for Juvenile Delinquent.

My unisex Scottish-Gaelic handle wasn't amidst kids' name signs in stores or among any conversation class appellations. *Tout de suite* the misfit, Mademoiselle Whatchamacallit, translated to the moniker, Monique. Francophile Miss Apgar wasn't like any other teacher to cross our paths. As when this comely instructor wasn't conjugating, she was likely moonlighting for foundations and lingerie showrooms. Her killer legs belonged in Mary Quant's super short skirts, mini dresses, and micro shorts. My mother *kibitzed* her astonishment during her weekly yentathon.

Nineteen sixty-seven inaugurated the Summer of Love at Monterey Pop and propelled the burgeoning youthquake on both coasts. San Francisco and Cambridge surfaced as counterculture antipodes. Two thousand four hundred seventy-five feet from the eminent, but square, Harvard Business School, a triangular plaza in Cambridge transmogrified into a hub for questing artists, students, neophiles, and wannabes searching for a musical or narcotic hit. Eggheads and potheads converged in Harvard Square, evolving as the Aquarian Age axis for all that was hip and happening. Even the mighty Bob Dylan traveled from NY to Club Passim or Club 47 at 47 Mt. Auburn St., hellbent on performing or working there. Joan Baez and Muddy Waters were regulars at this consecrated folk hall. Literati and cineastes had a choice of nine theaters and a 24-hour Paperback Booksmith, specializing in history, philosophy, and anti-war volumes to calmative nightlong classic music. Boutiques sold esoterica like bongs, pipes, and psychedelic paraphernalia. A meal at Grendel's Den was all the more appetizing with its waitresses rustling in vintage granny dresses. Those of a certain age may salivate at the mere mention of Buddy's Sirloin Pit, Bailey's Ice Cream, Club Casablanca/Casa B., or even the Pewter Pot Muffin House.

John Phillips of the Mamas and the Papas wrote the sunny Scott McKenzie ballad, *San Francisco (Be Sure to Wear Flowers in Your Hair),* that began cross-pollinating staid suburbs like mine. Flower Power was in full bloom. Boisterous, rebellious children overrode this local purlieu, intent on catching the feeling and a few rays. Weekends were made for adopting a fictive self, sporting love beads and multicolored regalia, and departing bourgeois Belmont. I was on a mission, bivouacking to Brigham's Ice Cream in pursuit of my flavor penchant, mocha almond. Belmont Center had its franchise, but the Harvard Square location made it neat.

Parents could sanction such spare time gadabouts. The real game changers of this crisis year consisted of droves of runaways leaving their sheltered, middle class milieu. Between 1967 and 1971, a mass hegira of 500,000 adolescents flocked to experimental communities. Joan Didion encapsulated innocents swarming to Haight-Ashbury in her seminal, *Slouching Towards Bethlehem.* The Beatles' *She's Leaving*

Home probes parental bewilderment at the abrupt, quizzical disappearance of their daughter during this surge.

"I had everything money could buy—diamonds, furs, a car—but my father and mother never once told me they loved me," Melanie Coe, the real-life subject and tabloid topic of this Beatles song, substantiated. The most talked about film of the year, *The Graduate*, highlighted the disconnect between wealth and happiness as the generation gap widened.

Even greater social ruptures defined the long, hot summer. During the late '60's, race riots detonated across the nation, ravaging 159 major cities in a mere three months and leaving Newark and Detroit charred beyond recognition. Tempers flared on TV, at dinner tables, and unexpectedly in school corridor polemics. As hormones raged, so did heated opinions and opposing factions.

Heavy issues, to be sure, but just as weighty was our grand girdle grappling. At our mother's behest, my sisters and I were now armed and dangerous to ourselves, swathed in Playtex beneath our party frocks. Merely squeezing into this rubbery, constrictive support could induce hematomas. Gertrude flopped out of hers like a doomed fish writhing dockside in the open air.

The Freedom Trash Can served as a repository for girdles and other accoutrements of oppression at the notable feminist demonstration of the Miss America Pageant on September 7, 1968 in Atlantic City. To set the story straight, officials dissuaded protesters from igniting their undergarments since a receptacle poised on the wooden boardwalk risked inflaming the tourist attraction.

New York Post reporter, Lindsy Van Gelder, deliberated beforehand as to whether militants like draft dodgers would burn their bras? "If the average American woman gave up all her beauty products, she would look like Tiny Tim and there would be no reason for the American male to have anything to do with her at all," humorist Art Buchwald bantered as he promulgated this intimate apparel immolation mythology. His remark proved more incendiary than their actions. Appearing on live TV, a handful of intrepid women stood their ground at the pageant, elevating banners reading "Women's Liberation" and "No More Miss America."

Thus began The Battle of the Sexes on Saturday night in Anytown, USA. Television had such an addictive effect that some homes fashioned a viewing room or den. Family and friends congregated on capacious, bright-toned sectional couches contiguous to soothing wooden paneled walls for gradually more extended programming. Remotes didn't exist, so sitting close to the cumbersome set was key. And, mother, not being much of a cook, was the perfect foil, no cheap pun intended, for the much-heralded "Swanson Night," frozen prepared TV Dinners. We became the unofficial talking heads for these heat-and-eat meals. The *plat du jour* could be Morton's, Banquet's, or Chun King's, contingent on the grocery store's weekly sales flyer. To heighten their dining pleasure, viewers supped on metal patterned TV trays, in their laps, or perched on folding tables.

Lonely hearts could now partake of their very own dinner for one. Solitudinarians and schizoids had a respectable repast of, say, turkey with all the sides, when flying solo on Thanksgiving. Lance the blueberry muffin with a candle and partake of a solitary yet reliable, many happy returns.

My coming of age came and went in a uniform of saffron chiffon. Plucked from the rag trade bowels of Filene's, *Old Yeller* glossed a bevy of bar, bat mitzvahs, and *Birthday* parties. Whatever the occasion, my distress may have been from the steel boned corset, garter belt hooks, or the vacuous blather. I was usually much more attentive to the smorgasbord than to schmoozing. Making small talk isn't my strong suit, although outers and inners have become much more pliant over the years.

A pair of more innovative parents treated us to a Boston Harbor Cruise bat mitzvah blast. Agile adolescents were frugging and twisting in counterpoint to the ship's rocking and rolling movements on the upper deck. Others stood at the rail absorbing the sunshine, sea breeze, spray, and ongoing panorama of the Old North Church, Bunker Hill Monument, and other points of interest. A few huddled, enthralled with the rhythm of the momentary breaking waves and frothy white foam. A hypnotized roisterer, Kurt, made the ultimate sacrifice to King Neptune as, when leaning over, his wire rims landed in the drink.

Kurt's loss of property was minor compared with my own gustatory gaffe. One crisp autumn afternoon, Beth El Temple's teens got together for a hayride and pizza. My middle school motormouth masticated at full speed ahead. "It's a bird!" "It's a plane!" It's a mozzarella comet kerplunking in Carrot Top's (Elvin's) cola cup. Things go better with Coke, but this wasn't one of them. Jared tried turning a blind eye. Both were unruffled, but my chagrin festered. Without an etiquette monarch such as Emily Post, Ann Landers, or Ask Beth to consult, wailing was the only recourse. I could not rely on my usual schizoid receding as this pair would be in class.

Sometimes I devised coping mechanisms. I credit Jody of the rump ruckus as a catalyst to contriving a new way of entering a crowded room—,crabwise—,as a diversion sparing me from becoming, ahem, the butt of any more of her and her fangirls' jokes.

My ponderous gawkiness was mostly encumbering to me. An asphyxiating sense of inadequacy, Gertrude's perfectionism, and tangible ungainliness around others enshrouded me. Jared and Elvin have no recollection of that episode, time notwithstanding, and we remain faithful, if infrequent, consorts. This twosome and maybe even most of mankind allow for being human to a greater extent than my mother would. Fortunately, my table manners have ameliorated in spite of present trends.

Who would have ever thought that the "King of Cool," Steve McQueen, would come to Belmont Country Club? *Bullitt* buzzed as the year's box office smash. Lights, camera, action. Our pinup playing golf, (*A Sucker Bet)* practically in our own backyard. Norman Jewison's *The Thomas Crown Affair* was filmed locally in Boston, Cambridge, Ipswich, South Hamilton, and preternaturally on our turf. In awe, my sisters and I contemplated the set and numerous takes from a respectful distance. We were surely starstruck. The 301st most-popular all-time person exuded style, sexuality, and swashbuckling in spades.

Forty-six Country Club Lane: where heretofore nothing more earth-shattering than unearthing the front yard had occurred. Suddenly, Paul Newman's rival spiced up the fairway. My thoughts began to run wild. By a twist of fate, I could come across either the Hood milkman delivering glass bottles or a movie idol. Heading out and having my usual panty bag or stocking snag coupled with a smidgen of serendipity. The cosmic possibilities were mind-boggling.

The greatest contribution of 1968's musical renaissance was that songs informed the listener with more consciousness and meaning than ever before. Their lyrics resonated even more profoundly for mavericks who melded with their "special" or "only friend" (The Doors' *When the Music's Over*) to amend for their sidelining and inner turmoil.

Some crooners addressed taboo topics with a risqué smattering of double entendres. The Doors' *Love Me Two Times,* my favorite, is one such number. Flamenco bassist Robbie Krieger's poignant ditty recounts a sailor or soldier bidding farewell to his girlfriend or wife before shipping off to Vietnam. At a blushing 18, on his first-ever attempt, he composed *Light My Fire*. What were most of us doing at that tender age?

The country's involvement in controversial Vietnam was the foremost theme, and songs skewed to partisanships: "Hawkish," *Sgt. Barry Sadler, The Ballad of the Green Berets* or "Dovish," *Country Joe and the Fish, I Feel Like I'm Fixin' to Die Rag.*

Recording artists rejoiced in rampant sex and drugs experimentation as de rigueur for their heady, high-risk lifestyles. Janis, Jimi, and Jim all flamed out prematurely, becoming canonized members of the notional 27 Club, a pantheon of popular performers, lost way too soon at one score and seven years. Their ephemeral incandescence served as an advisory of the perils of out-of-bounds hedonism, the dark side associated with the era's permissiveness.

Mother was sculpting more these days, returning home replete with anecdotes about another class participant, microbiologist Salvador Luria's snakes. This asp man would soon be part of a Nobel Prize-winning team (Physiology or Medicine, 1969, viral genetics and replication mechanisms).

While her busts gathered dust, she rallied her daughters to dabble as dilettantes. So art for art's sake it was, and off I went with not a piddling concern in the world.

The aroma of fresh mowed grass is always invigorating, but especially so for the memories stirred by summers spent at deCordova Sculpture Park and Museum. The 30-acre complex framed a children's camp that stimulated alfresco expressiveness and camaraderie. This Lincoln park reigned as the most extensive and agrarian in New England.

That MetroWest township, merely 9.2 miles away from ours, was decidedly more rural with its unfettered public conservation land, rock crops, rambling estates, and pond-fringed properties. Modern architects began calling this sylvan area home.

The Walter Gropius House (Harvard educator and a founder of The Architects Collaborative), put the town on the map. Although "modest in scale...revolutionary in impact," this edifice is open to the public and worth a gander.

Cows peered listlessly from split fence rails at intermittent camping motorists. And a true sign of the times, a mammoth hand-painted peace symbol flag draped the broad side of a barn bespoke only one possible side to the conflict.

Master portraitist Fred Petroskey taught our painting class, guiding with a precision and empathy that I had never experienced in my grade school classes. And although he was substantially older, then in his thirties, his instruction never felt patronizing. Had I been of legal age, I would have wanted Fred to be my drinking partner, but still being a minor, I settled for inking instead.

DeCordova provided a continual, scintillating cast of characters. Sometimes we meet someone who will change the course of our destiny. Blond, lithesome Valeria was that person. The Rolling Stones had just issued their seventh studio album, *Beggars Banquet*, marking a distinct departure from their earlier psychedelic pop and trending more toward a blues rock sound. The band's fan base and appeal skyrocketed as the decade drew to a close.

Many girls leched after Mick Jagger's bad boy image. The Beatles wanted to hold your hand; the Rolling Stones wanted to hold (you fill in the blank). Patently, it wasn't so much the outpouring of tunes; it was the soloist Valeria idolized.

She rhapsodized over every detail of "The Glimmer Twins," Mick and Keith, with a contagious ardor. I soon became her factotum as we ransacked underground fanzines, hanging a shingle as our own outtasight, teenybopper clipping service. Post-Valeria, at the advanced age of twenty-one, I persevered with my Mick scrapbook packed securely in my childhood room while on semester breaks from college. One fateful night, my father barged in unannounced and caught me *in particeps criminis*, snipping and taping. "You're too old for that," he scoffed backpedaling.

My zest for the band has waned, but my passion for their heyday music remains unwavering. Travel to the ionosphere with Mick Taylor's exquisite solo in *Sympathy for the Devil* 4:20, live at Madison Square Garden, on *Get Yer Ya-Ya's Out!:The Rolling Stones in Concert*. I rest my case. As for Valeria, I can't say whether she continued her education, but of this much I'm certain, she would have made an Ivy League groupie. And I might have the papers to prove it.

Chapter 5

Hair Today,
Gonzo Tomorrow

Love-ins, be-ins, sit-ins, and believe it or not, a honeymoon bed-in with John and Yoko taking an acquiescent, peacenik stance between the sheets and becoming the original forerunners of the staycation. Boundaries were eroding, and sexes sometimes appeared indistinguishable from a distance. Protest art or tie-dye was all the rage, with swirls, patterns, and colorations as individualistic as the wearer. During the '60's, Rit Dye was on the brink of bankruptcy, but their shrewd marketer, Don Price, stewarded the company's changeover from boxed to squeezable rainbow colors with the foresight to fund artists to produce hundreds of tees for the upcoming

Woodstock Festival. Without these hordes of grungy hippies as customers, Rit Dye would have lost its shirt.

Even Gertrude followed the groove in blue and white blotched putter pants while we looked after the hibiscus and rhododendrons out back. All could emulate a far out lifestyle if only avocationally. Attending a matinee performance of avant-garde, *Hair the Musical,* Mother and I again found ourselves in the thicket of it all, sitting in the front row during the highly publicized naughty, naked, nude finale.

Hair captured the zeitgeist, although this production now seems very dated. Back in the day, our crowning glories made far greater statements than today. Hoydenish vanity excused Lorna flaunting falls and wigs in blatant artifice. Classmate Serena compared Diavola's nappy, raven scalp to poodle fur. Gertrude chided my unkempt Sheepdog, like the rest of my persona, as an invariant mess. In desperation, I ironed my mane to achieve Cher-like sleekness. Some of *Seventeen*'s circulation relied on drug store hair straighteners, but for all hippiedom's ascendancy, few were willing, in the words of Lennon-McCartney, to *Let it Be.*

The Doors' *Hello I Love You* cued me that in spite of all my industry, I would never possess what those *Foxy Lady* statuesque lookers did—long, attenuated legs— and how much both sexes dug them, particularly as skirts grew shorter. "The girls girl-watchers watch, drink Diet Pepsi," the buzzword blared. Schizoids watch out for such unwanted advances.

Yardley introduced "Next to Nothing" compacts as their way of gilding the lily. My first lipsticks, Dollys, were orange, pink, and white striped tubes encompassing subtle glosses. On the cusp of womanhood, smearing this nacreous hue would elicit the next big first, a kiss.

The set nestled in hand. I surmised my mother purchased this gift as my father often scorned such adornment and eye shadows, in particular, as buffoonish. If the counterculture had a natural beauty enabler, it was Dad.

Like father, unlike daughter. Applying cunningly, then obliquely, now became my trademark, *Red Badge of Courage.* Of course, being schizoid, I gave zip thought to that first big, moist, junior high smacker, hoping to look somewhat better than my then maladroit appearance. Experimenting with the inventiveness, not the sensuality, of the palette.

School bombinated with the birds and bees as contemporaries began to see the opposite sex through new eyes. So did I. After viewing *Planet of the Apes* at Fresh Pond Cinema, packs of mulleted jocks gamboling pell-mell modified into simians out of Central Casting.

"Boy, is this kid handsome," Gertrude gushed to Aunt Rita as we neared the Finnish clothier Marimekko in Harvard Square. "He's tall, slim with auburn hair and brown eyes. You know, huge, smoldering ones, like Omar Sharif's!" Mother didn't exaggerate, as Donny was all that and seasoned well beyond his years. A cardiologist's son, this Belmont Hill School student, had definitely sampled the seamier side of life.

"You're a real cutie," Donny spoofed a transvestite's come-on to me. His swish, light in the loafers, parody jarred with his own seductive zinger, "Cast your petals while you're young," he wheedled. I wouldn't, but how did he become so jaded?

Then one day, Donny no longer attended private school. Out of the blue, he appeared at Belmont High. Hanging around Claypit Pond, he had lost his magnetism, looking downcast and dissipated instead. Whispers in the corridors of cocaine, marijuana, and heroin enveloped him. Rumors ran rife with reports he OD'd in his bedroom. Dead, another casualty of the Age of Aquarius. "He was bent on self-destruction," Gertrude cried out, "And don't flatter yourself. You couldn't have saved him." She stumbled on Donny curled up, bawling, and utterly distraught one morning. "Are you alright?" she sympathized. In a microsecond, my mother knew he would never live to be seventy.

"Life's a funny thing, you know. And nobody wants to get old, but they don't wanna die young either," The Human Riff philosophized. (From the documentary, *Keith Richards: Under the Influence*, 2015).

Classmate Ray, an exemplary towheaded 4-H Club (a community-minded organization expounding a Positive Youth Development Movement with Head, Heart, Hands, Health endeavors) and Youth in Action innovator, would turn to my desk, adopting an expression of mock revulsion. "Eew, glasses and braces!" he would snigger. Boomers procured orthodontia their forebears couldn't earmark for themselves. My dental hygiene came short of the scrupulously clean that the practitioner recommended.

Although an esteemed Center establishment, Dr. Fleck had his own questionable procedures, such as cleaning my braces and transferring the detritus to my visage. Gertrude got into his face for what he left on mine. "Did they teach you that in dental medicine school?" she inveighed.

Under or overbite, south to Cushing or west to Waverly, this sedate childhood usually boded shelter from such indignities, and yet, my unorthodox orthodontist was a jolting brush with one very basic fact of life: the world was divided into the insane and those I hadn't met yet. "You don't deserve such perfect teeth," Dr. Fleck teased as he bussed me. I had to hand it to this "professional" after being dealt a sad hand.

Belmont subbed as a byword for well-being, like-mindedness, and sophistication for its mostly well-heeled townies. Even the Center's market, Sage Grocery, offered curated goods displayed more stylishly than the more discounted, comparable offerings at competitive food chains. Prior to 1900, the founder, Edwin R. Sage, Sr., began his career as a farmer by trade, marking his fellowship with the area's original tillers of the field.

The town's lure lies in its accessibility to Cambridge and

Boston while fully retaining its georgic appeal. MIT and Harvard had campuses a mere bike ride away. Professors' offspring dotted my classrooms, with some of the more precocious taking college-level courses. This upper crust deck was clearly stacked against me and my academic hindrance.

The world seemed to spin out of control at this supercharged time. The globe erupted while my parents faded—the perfect storm for teen havoc. The vulnerable will veer toward manipulators in lieu of genuine nurturance. Domestic instability exacerbated my already diminished attention span. "What's wrong?" genial German instructor, Mr. Penta, casually inquired.

My grades began spiraling down with my class participation growing negligible. Sometimes I omitted assignments altogether and seemed befuddled. Preoccupied, he may have surmised I was stoned. Sex, and drugs, and rock and roll, proclaimed the mantra of the day. My abulia, regrettably, was natural.

"She's so out of it," Lorna's pre-pre-med date, Harvey, gibed as if I were a sideshow freak in a *Purple Haze*.

To a puzzled Mr. Penta, the only languid response I could summon was denial or an ineffable disclaimer for the all too salient. The truth is, I didn't have a pat answer for him or for anyone else. Even myself. Those with personality disorders often don't sense something's awry. And whether at school or at home, nobody willingly broached the elephant in the room.

Puerile dependency made splitting my miserable home a pipe dream. Our German Shepherd, Schatz, was also a flight risk. He regularly made a run for it, hightailing to the greener pastures of adjacent Lexington. My mother did what any ex-New Yawka would do and called a cab to retrieve him. Their hack driver, dog-tired of his tussles with this obdurate pooch, refused the fare.

School was out, and so *The Addams Family* would

travel abroad. Even before learning our itinerary, my gut reaction was, must we? Our prior attempt at togetherness, sharing a hotel suite at the Expo (International and Universal Exposition) '67 in Montreal, was a fiasco. Diavola fulminated against my father's *Kareishu* (Japanese for elderly smell), that malodorous mélange of "candle wax, aged cheese, and old books." She grumbled that his nonenal nuked our quarters and clamored for separate lodgings. Her newfound olfactory sensitivity was inconsistent with her deep-seated elation in bodily emissions.

The '60's marked the apex of the creative advertising revolution when jingles became household words, and industry executives partook of saturnalian three-martini lunches. "I made a fresh new discovery," Diavola lampooned a commercial's tagline as her euphemism for flatus.

Great Britain. I fortified myself for the next go. If only I could produce a doctor's note exemption, but then my doctor-father was underwriting this jaunt. Going, going, gonzo.

Little did I know that playwright, Brendan Behan, had been a goner for five years when we saw *The Quare Fellow* in Dublin. But we wouldn't have known of his real-life incarceration, bisexuality, or understood too many nuances of its depiction of impending capital punishment. More inmate or soul mate?

Later, intent on reading Behan's self-description in English class, relaying his own words with a brogue, I vocalized his despondency, "I know I present a comical figure." An anti-hero *The New York Times* eulogized as "The brawling, the boisterous, the antic were themes of his life and his work." I did so with a braggadocio as surprising to me as to the others present.

World Wind Tours #225 guide Charlie Cartwright (Ian McShane) in the film *If it's Tuesday, This Must be Belgium* was the only Brit we had ever heard call any female, "Luv."

Addressing us so sweetly and in such lilting accents was as winning off-screen as it was in that travelogue romance.

Our United Kingdom trip had many striking moments, as when my shutterbug father photographed about all the tartans tacked in every conceivable spot in a Highlands inn so that seeing would be believing. Simple, solitary pleasures like collecting seashells and broken porcelain shards in Galway Bay or gathering heather in Tyndrum returned as sentimental reminders. We even journeyed to Blair Castle in the village of Blair in Perthshire, Scotland, and I finally felt at home with my nettlesome name.

We never coalesced, abroad or at home, ambling in separate directions: my father to his camera shops, my mother to her high-end cultural attractions, and we mods to the epicenter of hipness, London's Carnaby Street. The glue that holds us together didn't bind.

Back across the pond, the daily grind got Gertrude taking driving lessons not just to recoup peripatetic Schatz but because she was more community-minded. *The Times They Are A-Changin'*, above all. Mom wasn't keen on being my practical joker father's front seat passenger since he would close his right eye, feigning sleep while on the highway knowing how high-strung she was. (Another ruse at the office, he would circulate the waiting room with a jar of surgical goat eyes soliciting donations.) Dad tried to teach mom to ride a bike utilizing training wheels, but she would leap off within the driveway. All the same, she managed to get a license and went about her to-do list.

They were a heterosexual mismatched redo of the year's comedy winner, Neil Simon's *The Odd Couple* but without the gags.

The his and hers of compact cars: Dad's Dodge Dart and Mom's Chrysler Plymouth Valiant. Both were proponents of consumer activist Ralph Nader, whose visionary, *Unsafe At*

Any Speed reformed the auto industry, reducing fatalities by 80 percent and saving 3.5 million lives, as the keynote in *The Nation, How Ralph Nader Changed America*. His bestseller tweaked Congress to pass legislation and President Johnson to sign into law the creation of the National Highway Traffic Safety Administration.

Gertrude would never pardon hitching even in serene Belmont, and so she offered a ride to my classmate, David, a free-spirited, no holds barred soul. Passing chiseled yards while exchanging pleasantries, the drive went without incident until that troublous topic intervened. Vietnam, was the first televised war and the most contested word in our collective lexicon. No one could remain neutral, not even anchorman Walter Cronkite, "the most trusted man in America."

My veteran mother and firebrand guest had expectedly antithetical views, consequently I steeled myself for an inflammatory confab while bracing for a possible collision. "Fighting for peace is like fucking for chastity," mild-mannered David boldly announced.

Gertrude slammed on the brakes, tires screeching, threw open the Valiant's backseat passenger door, and threw out David. A Bohemian babe right back into the woods.

And then she trounced. Her tirade was ear-splitting, merciless, and only beginning. This inopportune altercation left ample time for her to regroup for the Hubs' return from work and a renewed assault. What on earth? He said it, we didn't do it, but no matter.

Gertrude adhered to a take no prisoners approach to miscreants and the potty-mouthed alike.

Even peach fuzz could be moot. Men in the making wallowed in the daily appearance of a few new follicles. One coaxed me to validate his virility and stroke some almost indiscernible whiskers. In his younger days, impish Billy had played with a lighter with still visible burn marks from that horrendous incident. I tried to ignore his cheek's disfigurement as I warily patted the down.

We ducked behind the tool shed fully clothed, but Gertrude became extremely suspicious that we were fondling more than stubble. She sent her minion, Lorna, to investigate and put the kibosh on this underage activity.

Facial hairs today, Billy gonzo tomorrow.

Gertrude disapproved Sydney's greeting his patients in the waiting room. "What's wrong with that?" her brother, George, piped up.

On an otherwise unremarkable weekend day, *The Addams Family* headed to the office. A main floor staircase led upstairs to a teensy antechamber bounding our former apartment. That slight vestibule served as an employee lounge with a usually stocked refrigerator.

Mother detected more than putrefying takeout on this visit. Gertrude gleaned turpitude, the stench of moral decay. She found her evidence in a stash of *Playboys*, some with unfurled centerfolds strewn on the cube table. Hugh Hefner, his decadent clubs, their wild parties, and pneumatic Bunnies of the Swinging Sixties defiled the workplace. A reprobate optometrist lurked in our midst, in aptly named Ball Square.

My mother's *weltanschauung* skewed to absolutes: The War, that mother-in-law, Blanche, or my cronies.

We grew up to the tune of an all-encompassing God (*He's Got the Whole World in His Hands*). Yet a schizoid's sphere of influence also cleaves black and white, lacking whole object relations or the ability to glean integrated positive and negative qualities in others. (Elinor Greenberg, PhD, "What Everyone Ought to Understand about Schizoid Personality Disorder." *Psychology Today*, October 17, 2020.)

Our Mother Earth positively popped in resplendence. Astronaut William Anders' Christmas Eve photograph,

Earthrise, taken with a Hasselblad onboard Apollo 8 (1968), shows a stunning, blue orb against the sheer blackness of space. Of this rhapsodic image from 250,000 miles away, Mission Commander Frank Borman waxed effusive, "It was the most beautiful, heart-catching sight of my life...the only thing in space that had any color to it. Everything was either black or white, but not the Earth."

Five hundred thirty million people gazed, enraptured with the summer televised moonwalk on Sunday, July 20, 1969. President Kennedy's pledge (May 25, 1961) to attain a lunar landing by decade's end was near fulfillment. Contentious factions cohered in their entrancement of the heroics of the Apollo 11 Eagle module mission. To my mother, witnessing Neil Armstrong and Edwin Buzz Aldrin's two-hour exploration was beyond historic or chauvinistic; its magnitude made it sacrosanct. All other Sorrel activities would be suspended for strict up-to-the-minute observance of this milepost.

We girls sat dutifully glommed to the TV except for those pesky nature calls. Gertrude even took a moratorium from her paperwork. Such was the gravitas of this momentous broadcast.

Out of nowhere, heels clicked in a crescendo on the walkway. Hmm... Gertrude shot a withering glance at the front door. Whispering, she ordered us to crouch down in the airy den, remaining stock-still, until the intruders left. Her girlfriend, Shirley Glickman, with her giggly daughters, was not as over the moon with this spectacle and, having nothing better to do, dropped by.

Armstrong dignified this interplanetary conquest in his pithy "small step for a man" on Tranquility Base, which coincided with a housewife's misstep at 46 Country Club Lane, one which the lady of the house chose to sidestep, all synchronized by the light of the moon. Lunaticus, that medieval malediction, had suckerpunched our nation on a gripping eve that capped the climax of this restive eon.

Space shuttles and astronauts were now "in." And fashion designers toed the line with silver pants and chain mail (Courreges, Cardin, Rabanne), films (*Marooned*), and moonstruck songs. Even Revlon formulated an affordable Moon Drops lipstick line for a fashiony, futuristic twinkle. And last but not least, Frank Zappa dubbed a daughter, Moon Unit.

The biggest event ever eternalized David Bowie's *Space Oddity*, Steve Miller's *Space Cowboy,* and The Beatles' *Across the Universe,* all released that year and with many more lunar-loving tunes to come. Stanley Kubrick's *2001: A Space Odyssey* accessorized craning, futuristic necks with a Wells' The Monolith gemstone pendant. Space cadet, space shot, and spacing out became contemporary slang that contemns my schizoid stupor. U.S. aeronautics achieved an unprecedented, space race high while touching down with a new parlance low.

Chapter 6

That '70's Schizoid Show

The terminal year of this extraordinary decade climaxed with some final acts and fearsome headlines. Most quailed at the gruesome Sharon Tate murders in August 1969, affright at their sheer senselessness and brutality. The Beatles gave their last performance on Apple Records' roof. Jim Morrison battled indecency and profanity charges that decimated The Doors to the backdrop of a nation growing more rabidly conservative. And come December 6th, the free concert the Rolling Stones bestowed as a holiday present to fans, "The West Coast Woodstock," at Altamont raceway, sunk into a Hells Angels rampage, leaving a corpse onstage. This macabre denouement dashed the utopian dream once and for all.

The '60's afterglow dimmed as social issues petered from flames to embers.

"Turn off that noise," my parents barely communicated with me except for that other generational censure. This juvenile sound barrier spoke volumes more about how little we conversed.

The Blaschka Brothers produced 4400 phenomenal glass botanical models of 800 plant species bestriding the Harvard Museum of Natural History. Liquid sand stunned as sublime, uncannily authentic plants that sprouted a Sabbath sanctuary for my mother.

The Glass Flowers functioned as her refuge from my father as the traditional Day of Rest sometimes retrogressed into a Day of Redress. Hurtling down the tortuous squiggly slide at Beaver Brook Reservation State Park would have better defused the tensile aftereffects. At any rate, separate Sundays in this world-class greenhouse shrine were preferable to the strident interplay between my parents. And why wouldn't Sydney apply to Mass General already and appease Gertrude?

Where there is discord, there is divorce, but it wasn't as sanctioned then, and Dad had more fundamental decency than to abandon a mother of three. "You have an absentee father," my good-natured Aunt Rita fessed up. Her husband, George, and his big sister, Gertrude, were inseparable during their stopovers from Bayside, so I speculated if she also felt excluded. Mom was his "mentor, his confidant, his ad hoc mother" with an affinity and adoration I had never shared with my sisters.

Yet my Bayside kin was a demonstrative couple visibly attentive to their daughters. "Make nice," Rita clucked her motto and M.O. (*modus operandi*). The architect and fine artist exhausted Bearskin Neck's studios agog at the nautical oils.

Uncle George and "Ri" with their younger girls, arrived in time for dinner. Their frail middle girl, Lisa, most resembled her father and, like him, shadowed my mother. She spent hours alone with Gertrude, almost becoming her disciple. Part of her allegiance was reverence, and part was foreboding.

Most little kids fear the monster under the bed. Lisa wept in terror of the one in the next bedroom—an overaged thumb sucker who would remove her pollex only long enough to brutalize her.

Gertrude excoriated that "wicked child" and, being protective of Lisa, spurred her to spend time with me instead. "Blair is kind and supportive and would never treat you that way," she advocated. In lieu of a brown bag lunch, we rehearsed a skit from a few random items in a sack. My cousin dried her eyes. She may not have become my follower that day, but she's remained loyal.

Filene's Basement's Frosty Corner became the subterranean cranny where my mother and I warmed to each other. After epic hunter-gathering, we relished the specialty of the house; a soft serve vanilla cone sprinkled with malted milk in a paper cornet. We communed in silence over our treasures and dairy twists.

"Filene's was the archetype of the mother. It always gave you something—good gifts, good deals, and good bargains." (Manon Merchand, *Final Markdown for Filene's Basement.* Suzanne Kreiter, *Boston Globe*, December 30, 2011.)

Most area shoppers knew that about Downtown Crossing's The Basement. Surplus, overstock, or closeout, they all spelled decked out. Maybe we would even get them on their final 75 percent off markdown. New York had its Ladies' Mile and so did its country cous, Boston. The big three: Raymond's "Where You Bot the Hat," more downmarket Gilchrest's, and Dollar Days' gloating Jordan Marsh; Washington Street, the real Combat Zone of fistic females buying and Running Brides trying their trousseaux.

Pre-Project Runway, my mother copied The Blonde Venus, Marlene Dietrich's signature illusion style. Confounding that this screen siren, far more envied for her legs than her face, was usually cloaked in full-length evening clothes or menswear?

We were selecting junior sizes now with more figure-flattering lines in velvet and satin. Gertrude chose my amorphous champagne blouson style dress to cover a multitude of sins. Meself more a Jordan Marsh blueberry muffin top than a mannequin-like Marsha Jordan Girl. Ma made her illusion in cinched lace recalling a maiden aunt's handkerchief.

Lustrous fabrics transformed us into little lady ingenues, even if only at the Temple's dining hall. We would be the belles of this ball with my mother's wish to oversee our own such celebrations. On Halloween, she dressed us in native garb from mementos cadged on their travels. Hobbling in those authentic hand-painted Dutch wooden *klompen* substantially reduced the take-home booty.

Mom eagerly watched for some of her Sisterhood entourage, especially Bernice Bixon. Both primped and dabbed their wrists in synchrony. Bernice's Oriental Shalimar fused with Gertrude's floral White Shoulders.

Bernice was her complement and could have been an understudy for Melanie Wilkes in *Gone with the Wind* (Gertrude was temperamentally more Scarlett O'Hara.).

Melanie always did the right thing, and so did Bernice. She arrived clutching a tissue wrapped, still moist oil painting of pansies, a gift she made expressly for the occasion.

Yet Bernice's eldest, Alaina, held Gertrude as her role model during this era of homemakers. "I remember in high school how much I admired your mother. She was independent, original, intellectual, and talented. I liked the way she dressed and how different she was from most Belmont matrons."

"I remember meeting your mom in the '60's. She was at our back door. I had never met, at that period in my life, a person so unaffected and natural. Her hair was not beauty-parlored. Her eyes were fervent. In my memory, she had been working in some plantings and brought some for my mom. She has lived in a vivid moment of memory of meeting a person who was so real and present," her younger daughter Karen (now Alissa) recounted.

"Aunt Gertrude was hands-down one of my favorite people. Gertrude was a paragon of virtue and a force to contend with. This was not only because she could twist and break open an apple with her bare hands and break it into perfect halves, which was an incredible sight, but she was a competent nurse like my daughter, Jackie. Few individuals have impacted my life as dramatically as my Aunt Gertrude. Her energy, clear vision, and steadfast resolve in accomplishing tasks made her a powerful force. Gertrude's absolute certainty and idiosyncratic ways served to shape my core understanding of the world," niece, Lisa, enthused.

Alissa became the doctor my maternal grandmother wanted Gertrude to be (as did her sister, Ronda).

Television families were reinventing more credibly. Pristine and pearl collared, June Cleaver of *Leave It to Beaver* yielded to the bigoted good old boy, Archie Bunker of *All in the Family*. Mario Puzo's smash *The Godfather* made gangland drama mainstream, becoming a cultish movie blockbuster series. Reluctant son, Michael's (Al Pacino) assertion to his girlfriend (Diane Keaton), "It's my family, Kate, it's not me," hit home.

On the lighter side, Gertrude drove us to see the film version of the popular Broadway play, *Lovers and Other Strangers* with its extensive all-star cast. This comedy of adult themes preempted The Talk. I culled all I needed to know about it, exiting the theater cognizant that the fundamental difference between the sexes is that the ideal male coiffure smelled like raisins. My parents abstained, and their presumption was we probably should, too. The Angel of Asexuality did not pass over our house.

Belmont High supplemented this omission with Dr. Nicholas Fiumara's mandatory sex education presentation. The auditorium staged a slideshow of oozing, outsized genitalia and gross out gore. A renowned director of communicable maladies, his lecture relied on sensationalism to douse promiscuity's flame. Grabbing the mic, this clinician altered into a rabble-rouser for the itchy. "Here's one peeping at you… Tina's STD!" and "Yo, Clyde's syphilis," he bubbled over. Many students were what sociologists term familiar strangers. The good doctor afforded their nethers a familiarity that could only breed contempt, if not contamination.

Looming, homegrown naughty bits. Butt-ugly and better averted. "Blair's not looking, either," Audrey mouthed, shielding her eyes as she beheld me a few rows away, doubled over in repugnance.

The upshot: free love could come with a hefty price tag. And as with the Salem witch trials or his predecessor, Senator Joseph McCarthy of the infamous 1950's Red Scare, this zealot against sexually transmitted diseases, named names. Being the only Blair in town, I left the auditorium with no pragmatic knowledge whatsoever but quite relieved. That forbearing Angel spared me and my possibly pustulating privates from going public that day.

"That's what a body should look like," mother editorialized as Ali MacGraw flexed her perfect form in *Goodbye Columbus,* what Gertrude abominated about her anatomy, ditto and doubly so for mine. My God-given gams looked more like yams: turgid, unsightly, and mistakable for rejected, mutant produce. Or sometimes she borrowed girls' locker room grades nine through twelve-style invective for my honker, an all too ethnic banana nose, a distinguishing feature not heritable from her pixie and as prominent as Sydney's.

Schoolmates' physiques also surfaced on her unsolicited radar, often eliciting Puritanical reproval. Kaylee's biggish backyard flagrantly stressed the seam of her trousers, and her overgrown front yard posited a randy sophomoric tease. Gertrude nixed my intent to purchase a granny square crocheted vest as she detected a model's aureoles while wearing a similar garment in *Harper's Bazaar*. Not exactly what I had in mind but try arguing with her. I settled for the *Love Story* cloche hat and jeweled choker instead.

Icy waters still coursed New England veins. Moral gatekeepers, The Watch and Ward Society, and their draconian Banned in Boston censorship tenets restricted publications, plays, gambling, and prostitution until mid-century. By 1970, such prim constraints toned down and a Beantown nonprofit agency, The Women's Health Collective, released the respected tome, *Our Bodies, Ourselves*.

Kaylee arose as the first of my set to do it. She achieved womanhood and greater status by embellishing her deflowering narrative; a heads-up that her precursory priapus resembled what many housewives discarded unwrapped from the supermarket poultry section, a raw chicken neck.

This adventuress lolled on her sleeping bag, arching her neck and bare spine as an already accomplished exhibitionist in her early nudie cutie titillation phase. At our slumber parties, her two sidekicks, a pair of perky burlesque-bound nipples, made their accustomed cameo appearance.

Anyway, I matured, encased in library science, standard-issue, head-to-toe flannel, and with no real sense of my household being more repressed. Nor was I game for such dalliances; boys were just there. Saxophonist Clive's muttered coquetry and murmured blandishments were hardly music to my ears.

Interacting with these horny brethren was on the order of

how anthropologist Margaret Mead chronicled pubescence in her *Coming of Age in Samoa*. The only meaningful man in my life was Mister Magoo and the degenerative myopia we had in common.

Bell-bottomed and emboldened, pheromonal teens became more salacious in their utterances, if not their actions. Math-whiz, Jesse, took a first bite into the school lunch hot dog, devouring it with a gusto that suggested starvation. "Whose phallus are you eating?" a brazen Henry joshed. This soft-spoken Mr. Nice Guy emanated a subtle charm that made many girls confess to being twitterpated with him.

"Have you looked up Uranus?" reserved Aaron welcomed me to class. Coltish Mary Jane was running for class president on a totally forgettable campaign platform but with memorable signage emblazoned with sex in capital letters and the caption, "Now that I have your attention..." Bodacious Lindsay, whose curves bettered the school production as the lead in *The Impossible Years*, at times frolicked with panties as headgear.

Enter performing artist and heartthrob Lar Lubovitch, a veritable hunk among nerds. The more normal girls swooned and gurgled in his presence. Founded in 1968, his dance company was beginning to hit its stride, and to its credit, Belmont offered progressive cultural workshops.

Sitting on the sidelines, I watched with rapt attention as he nimbly raised a female aloft with the legerity of tossing a Frisbee. The ancients lionized discus throwers as gods. This visiting Adonis clasped and elevated the supple dancer with bravura. "I can't think of a single man who wouldn't want to hold a woman that way," the moderator praised.

Five decades later, his dance company has performed in every state of the country and in forty nations. *Variety* lauds Lar as a national treasure and the *New York Times* esteems him as one of the world's greatest choreographers. Even now, I think back to that spesh, shared moment in that modest classroom, a sweet spot in our sentimental education, when he was one of us. All these misty years haven't marred that pellucid image of a poised, triumphant ballerina. I wonder if she is still beguiled, tingling, reminiscing about his touch amid those callow hearts who also longed for it?

My parents' return from their gleeful European tour had a surprise ending. Joining them on this peregrination, were their wrong side of forty friends, Herschel and Rosalind, gung-ho about adopting an infant. Starting with Thomas Jefferson, Americans have had a long-term love/hate relationship with France.

This feckless couple didn't speak a word of French, but that didn't dissuade them from perambulating the outlying areas of the City of Light in pursuit of their heir apparent. And did they ever err! Awash with the intoxicating charm of this enchanting country as so many couples are, they somehow separated. Till death do us part...

The dutiful wife still proceeded to Orly Airport and their scheduled TWA departure. When Herschel's seat remained vacant, she concluded that the only plausible explanation for her spouse's absence was mortality. "When good Americans die, they go to Paris," Oscar Wilde quipped. Rosalind spent the next seven hours and twenty-three minutes in flight embroiled in funeral arrangements for her late husband. Herschel eventually surfaced and reunited with his aggrieved wife on this continent. But this near-death experience flew home as an often, restated choice souvenir from abroad. Akin to Sydney and Gertrude, childless Herschel and Rosalind, also seemed more harmonious.

Cinematic educators came across more like friends than pedagogues to their jejune charges. *To Sir With Love* and *The Prime of Miss Jean Brodie* were especially effective treatments.

English teacher, Mrs. B.J. Williams inherited the mantle. With her frosted nimbus and enameled daisy pins, she easily ranked as the office-holder for Most Popular among pupils. Her relaxed approach enhanced Tennessee Williams' *The Glass Menagerie* about socially anxious Laura's interiority. Then my class plodded through Richard Llewellyn's, *How Green was My Valley*. The plight of those indigent, Welsh mining families was foreign to kids reared on three squares and shag carpeting. While we followed the egregious Biafran-Nigerian civil war that made the nightly news, its imagery of Igbo genocide was too surreal to gauge.

Llewellyn's masterpiece, not youth, may have been wasted on us three green classmates. Jared, Elvin, and I would chortle and chaff in unison at our desks, a clandestine trio colluding with inside jokes. B.J. forewarned us she would dissolve this triangle, but united, we stood or sat even to this writing.

Mrs. Williams facilitated as a substitute sexual counselor while we leered between the lines when Huw Morgan initiated his heretofore flaccid chicken neck. Our winnings for soldiering on and studying this working class drama, a particularly prolix selection, I might add, on that ambitious high school punitive reading list, merited this actual hot part.

B.J. enjoined young Belmont bucks to pursue the dewy honeys in their midst as even her own daughter counted as one. "All mothers say theirs is a beauty," impudent Saul cracked wise. Unlike Jean Brodie, Mrs. Williams wasn't putting "old heads on young shoulders," but more worldly-wise ones.

A "double your pleasure, double your fun" kinda day with the two Williamses – B.J. and Tennessee. Neither that starry-eyed set piece nor *Time of the Season* was a compelling enough reason so I sat this one out. Remaining far more in my own little world than worldly-wise and as consensus had it, hard to read.

All the same, I performed adequately in school and sustained superficial friendships.

"I don't know what I'd do if something happened to my mother," alluring Serena agonized. Guiseppina was her best friend who even lent her glittery, polka dot cocktail sweater to her for a holiday party.

Classmate Diandra's mother found Serena's lookalike father totally irresistible. "He can park his boots under my bed," she mewled. Whenever he gave her the eye in *shul*, she imagined them entwined in erotic, bodice ripper high jinks. In the most inspired sexploit, this congregant/Lothario would ravage her while we were taking our pre-SATs, leaving her spread eagle and flushed with arousal on the stately mahogany dining table of their Queen Anne Victorian.

Susanna lured me from my quiet evenings at home to hers for Saturday night dinners downed with cosmopolitan *crème de menthe* and pineapple chunk cordials. Her feisty dad supplied them as we plied them along with his loquacious yarns.

Visiting others felt more like crossing customs checkpoints at limitrophes for entry to foreign lands. Poles apart, not for ethnic or decorative disparities, but more for the clubby vibe. Standard sights unseen at our residence: a mother beaming at her daughter and kissing her; a father enchanted by his child's chatter. Parental love permeated their countenances. As family members, we coexisted more like Eastern Bloc satellite states during The Cold War.

Andrea invited me to her home's traditional holiday open house. This memorable gathering occurred pre-commercialism, as Christmas really meant something in those days. Only the Hallmark Channel could have outshone such a gracious occasion. Singers Perry Como (*No Place Like Home for the Holidays*) and Jerry Vale (*Silver Bells)* furnished the accompaniment as diners' faces blushed with expectancy and ornaments dazzled. Whether family or friends, participants felt equally pampered with a sumptuous array of Italian delicacies.

Thumbing through yellowing photo albums, the dressier populace was significantly slighter than today, attributable to 10" plate portions, fewer processed foods, greater physical activity, and, yes, more smoking.

Some pageantry belies time and trends. I ran a Nausea Marathon gorging on biscotti, pizzelle, macaroni pizza, homemade eggnog, prosciutto, breadsticks, plus all manner of fried appetizers: artichokes, broccoli, cauliflower, veal, and chicken.

Breaking my own record in a non-competitive eating contest, I blobbed out on stuffed artichokes, sweet ricotta pizza, cookies, Panforte (Siena Cake), and cannoli while remembering to leave room for those roasted chestnuts

Surfeited, I slipped out—"Plopp Plopp Fizz Fizz"-ing Alka Seltzer—my two after dinner mints and antidote to unbridled esurience. Aside from Nonna's epic spread and its aftermath, this warm and fuzzy family had the real recipe for happiness.

Chapter 7

The Alphabet "Soup Nazi"

"Djeat?" "Dja," German teacher, Mr. Penta, overheard milling around in the hallways outside of his classroom. Translation: "Did you eat?" "Ya." While he may have parodied such contractions, this portly educator *sprechened* an acute or wicked hahd Boston accent. His pronunciation of Blair sounded much more like a bleating "Blay-ya." When Hanoi Jane (Fonda) was in town, he wanted to know, "Whe ya?" (Tufts University.) Monosyllables divided and conquered. An Eastern New England English native's patois is tough to neutralize.

As Somerville expats, we'd lose the swagger and regain

our final r's. Time for a new linguistic mentor. While mother and I were stickering frames during low-rated afternoon slots, we found our man. Patrician, persuasive, and with a pencil poised at his sesquipedalian mouth, Conservative Republican William F. Buckley, host of *Firing Line* and editor of *National Review,* would become my latest TV father and right hand man to ace the SAT vocabulary section.

At the Republican Convention in Miami in 1968, Mr. Buckley sparred with Gore Vidal (author of *Myra Breckinridge* and *The Best Man*) and caricatured himself with his teeth-baring comeback to his adversary. "Now listen, you, queer, stop calling me a crypto-Nazi, or I'll sock you in your goddamn face, and you'll stay plastered!" he glowered. Reason enough for me to be intrigued, as now anyone—but anyone—could lose his composure.

Comeuppance. We all have our stop calling me... nemeses. Touché to the hoi polloi who vilified me and my plurality of not having heads on our shoulders that we could summon his grace under frequent fire. On that firing line, we, the walking punch-drunk wobble, lifelong.

While other teens slurped ice cream floats or played intramural sports, I practiced a new hobby: weekend wordsmithery with William F. What I also developed in doing so was an emergent schizotypal or stilted speech pattern. Gertrude preened herself on my acquired skill set, even if it typecast me as all the more outlandish to my high school compeers *djeating* and *djaing* among themselves like some lingual lost tribe.

When it wasn't William F., it was Thomas Hardy, leading to other recondite and sometimes archaic phraseology. Anxiety gave rise to this logophile's formal delivery and, every so often, grandiloquence. Effete but also distancing for those less educated.

Exile on Blair Street produced periphrastic circumlocution

sometimes intelligible only to a party of one. "People don't talk that way," "Miss College Board," or "There's a fine line between erudition and dullness," was the motley reaction. The socially proficient adapt to the lingua franca of the listener to be more acceptable or fit in. Fitting in is not a schizoid watchword.

The thesaurus served as my trusty steed. *Merriam-Webster*, new partners in rhymes, supplied my midnight snack dog-eared on the nightstand. A literate night owl perusing etymologies until the rosy fingers of dawn.

Words were always there for you. Fun and educational too. As always, I had my own agenda.

My father and I swerved toward Arlington Center on a wintry night. I hoped we'd go to Luigi's for subs, but we stopped at a townhouse instead. An itty-bitty, red-headed housewife opened the door and led us into a small room revamped as her electrolysis studio. Dad needed to have his ears trimmed as patients noticed such matters. A greater chill consternated me as my mustache was about to become history. Hirsutism. Not a full-fledged specimen but a five o'clock shadow, nonetheless.

Sydney preceded me as my angst fomented. Next victim. The aesthetician moved deftly as she went about her *métier*. The heated, minuscule needle danced above my upper lip in fine pugilistic parries. Her fists channeled Cassius Clay, as they wafted in agile whorls, "Float like a butterfly, sting like a bee." The underdog, he entered the ring in Miami and defeated world heavyweight, Sonny Liston. "The hands can't hit what the eyes can't see," and then she tko'd my stash.

"Stand up straight! You're little enough!" (again ditto) Gertrude chastened. "Why didn't I give growth hormones to you?" as the actress and her idol, Suzy Parker, appeared on a talk show.

"I dunno. Why didn't you?" was my feeble plea.

Yikes! I committed another peccadillo, garbled enunciation, an additional demerit.

My stooping, irresolute slouch risked permanence. Serena's mother, Guiseppina, gestured to my hunched, humiliated, 45-degree angle. Prostrating myself as a Downward-Facing Sheepdog. You grovel girl! My mother's advisory that my abysmal posture would likely engender a slipped disc or pinched nerve fell on increasingly deaf ears, the classic schizoid deterrent.

Let bad hair days be bygones. The futility of taming the Jewfro or elflocks, panning my micromastia and other defects, reinforced my feeling like a moving target at a shooting arcade. Caught in the frequent crosshairs, my profile inclined before the put-downs and jibes as my self-worth all but eroded. In photos and in life, I seldom smiled.

The arthouse Brattle Theatre screened a spate of mind-bending movies. For Stones' fans, Donald Cammell and Nicholas Roeg's *Performance* showcasing Mick the Thespian was a must-see. Kaleidoscopic visions and cryptic Cockney jargon simulated hallucinogens; the diegesis, a concatenation of oddities reflected in a glass carnival funhouse mirror. Even the on-screen trysts could not surmount my reverie. I was well-embarked on my own schizoid course as imagination subverted concentration.

Prohibited from attending Woodstock, we teens had a Plan B in place. Kaylee, Serena, and I would set out for New York, Fun City, on our own. That is, until Gertrude learned of it. And true to form, she vowed to monitor us. Tittle-tattle circulated of how my strait-laced mother babysat on the Trailways bus. Grunting in the direction of my locker, the djeats and djas made known their most lowly monosyllabic opinion of me: dork. My head hung at half-mast.

Campbell Soup Company unfurled a poster campaign, "Turn your wall souper-delic." Gertrude did that, installing in my bedroom what is formally known to interior designers as Optical Square Black and White Illusion Wall Mural. Recast, informally known to me as which way to the vomitorium? And if I hadn't awakened from a bad trip before, I could count on awakening to one daily. A gyrating checkerboard called forth, "My wallpaper and I are fighting a duel to the death. One or the other of us has to go," ascribed to Oscar Wilde as his last words for future generations.

"...Work always lacks effort," "Just no interest whatsoever," "Inattention," "Disturbance," "Silly conduct," the teachers' remarks read. All those criticisms could have defined your scribe's output.

They are rather the report card marginalia of a class clown. Another outstanding pupil with an alleged 29 detentions in one year and an unbidden nuisance in class exhibitionism. No contemporary would have ever voted him Most Likely to Succeed, but he offered hope to those of us who will never graduate as Merit Scholars.

"The guitar's all right, John, but you'll never make a living out of it," his darling Aunt Mimi vented. In time, Lennon would be regarded as the nonpareil lyricist of his era.

Low achievement was inconsequential relative to his over the top talent and the astoundingly high musical compendium he gifted the anointed boomers and the fortuitous listeners to come. John had the adoration of his Aunt Mimi to compensate and keep him in check. The fact of the matter is, the verse closest to his heart acknowledged this simple truth, *All You Need Is Love*. Consider the jeerleaders and cheerleaders in your life, as they may very well determine its outcome.

The '70's resounded as a dilution of the '60's with a still distinct anti-establishment sentiment. Yet sweet sixteen, a stand-in cotillion, weathered the mayhem. Some mothers lavished victuals for my own little coming out as mine remained hospitalized on this tropical July afternoon.

My elusive father made an extemporaneous entrance. "Kaylee, your mother can cook for me anytime," Dad kvelled. His supervisory style plunked a finger in every pot. And then I watched incredulously as the other nine digits were suddenly wrapped around his toolbox. Never one to let grass grow under his feet.

So while we teens were scarfing down the recompense for a decade and six—staying on the straight and narrow throughout this groovy time—the head of the household started sanding the porch door. Undismayed pops resolved right then and there to replace its ragged screen. Returning moments later with his garage shop creeper, Sydney assumed a fetal position on the flagstone patio. Hammering to his heart's delight while we danced to ours and a medley of top ten tunes, he syncopated with a catchy—count 'em 1 per annum—16 beat rhythm. Dad was a session musician and sideman that juddering day.

"I don't want to go to camp," I demurred. My father swabbed the lens of a Nikon as I cravenly tiptoed into his study.

"Is that because you have your period?" he inquired. Speechless, I flushed the color of menses, orbs twitching. And no, that wasn't the uppermost reason, but I could not articulate the exact cause of my disinclination. *One is the Loneliest Number* for thee, not me.

That wrecking agent, withdrawal, deadened my dwindling desire for any group activities, even those deemed pleasurable. Yet camp contributed to versatility. Activities might bolster my applications. My grades would not guarantee admission to what my parents desired, a name school.

Entrance exams and an early call. Sydney dropped me off at the testing center by Claypit Pond with all the finesse of a newsboy hurling a periodical at a zonked out address. "Think!" he shouted, leaning out of the Dart's rolled down window before speeding off, leaving skid marks.

All those other kids sweated bullets as they pencil filled oval quiz answers. And there I was trying to slay the dragon of disassociation. The blurriness blunted my response time as my brain waged an uphill battle, torn between facts and fears.

Flagging focus and motivation did not make this schizoid much of a pedant. Not the nitwittery of the past, not Honor Society of the present, and unlikely any kudos in the future. While my sororal equals predetermined their rightful stead at The Seven Sisters' colleges, I envisaged mine as an *éminence grise* to reigning rock stars, their indispensable aide-de-camp in hot pants. Mick and Keef would confer VIP seating in their private plane, relying on me as their adroit linchpin when Truman Capote, Lee Radizwell, and other hangers-on wore thin.

Before jet-setting and transmuting to a boldfaced name, I would, however, board a bus for a seemingly interminable ride disembarking in decidedly less glam Bar Harbor, Maine. Eight hours and eighteen minutes of motion discomfort and Downeaster riffraff chucking glass soda bottle grenades at the unsuspecting driver (he pulled over at one point), we arrived at the campgrounds, an imposing Cottage Era 28-room waterfront villa with majestic Acadia National Park as its locus.

École Arcadie, a co-educational summer school, was set on nine acres with its own pond and a private deepwater dock. Mandatory French made me *mal a l'aise* (ill at ease). The bedwetting of Camp Pembroke begat another disquiet since, aside from spotty language command, I dreaded spotting. (Diavola labeled those bloodied dribs and drabs that sullied sanitary napkins as "slugs.")

Would La Directrice expose me and my slugs, with a foreign tongue lashing, one that I hardly spoke, let alone understood—that is, if I could pay attention long enough...

Would its property owner, Dr. Richard Gott, follow in my tracks?

I derived some comfort in knowing that Audrey was also attending, so I had the relief of her familiar, fair face.

Waking up to spectacular conifers and a refulgent Mt. Desert Island denoted halcyon days. The nearby blue nose ferry played reveille as it set sail for Nova Scotia every morning. Saltwater afternoon swims and rubbing elbows with a bonafide DuPont successor heightened its bonhomie.

École mollified the rigors of Francophilia by screening a recent release on Saturday night. New Wave Movies of the 1960's—seventh heaven for any film buff— mitigated our fumbling with this language of love.

We had mixers, too, with the neighboring niche camps, one for remedial reading and the other for golf (the stutterers and putterers). And we could explore the town's quirky local *tchotchke* merchants on weekends.

Yet even in this beauteous backwoods, I decompensated and, after brabbling with my roommates, escaped the fireplace appointed dormitory room to recuperate with my more sympathique acquaintance, Carlotta Virgin. (*Mais oui*, that was her real surname.)

"*L'enfer, c'est les autres,*" the monumental Philosopher-King, Jean-Paul Sartre, weighed in. Hell is other people. Preach it, brother, to the schizoid choir.

The meanies reimagined us besties as honorary lesbians. Our tête-à-tête wasn't the fling that Frank Sinatra's number one album *Strangers in the Night* intimated. (Ironically, "Ol' Blue Eyes" despised this torch song as being about "two fags in a bar" and often changed the lyrics.) Carlota remedied my post-traumatic from Mick's media circus marriage to Bianca in St. Tropez in May. Unlike most, she accepted me, warts and all sorts of weirdness.

Audrey held court at Belmont High, relating how she spent

her summer vacation with a particular side note exemplifying my campsite peculiarities to a disclaiming Amy. Gertrude met me at the bus station, my evident buffness long before Mireille Carillon's *French Women Don't Get Fat*, such a *mechaye*! Brandishing a report card, things went south. I blanched as her initial warmth degraded into a cold snap without her mincing words. "What happened?" she demanded to know.

Chapter 8

Rock And Roll High School

Colleen Corby was a model for many teens, and, in fact, a teen model, the face of the '60's and '70's. Rearranging my closet at the start of each new semester was orchestrated with her in mind, if not body.

A military detail that became a Belmontian nisus of assembled outfits and coordinated accessories granted barracks' precision. Spit and polish during peacetime, presumably. Operation Organize had its limited shelf life.

Gertrude's second self, Bernice, had a prepossessing daughter, Ronda, who never repeated an outfit. We nickered and neighed our yeahs to this one-trick clothes horse.

Snared in a muddle of mangled hangers, showstopping Colleen looked over my shoulder from the array of tear sheets encircling me. Contemporaries recognized her from the ubiquitous catalogs, editorials, and even TV commercials as a better iteration of themselves. She and her equally photogenic sister, Molly, were *it girls* before million dollar contracts. Hot babes had luminous complexions and full-blown hair upon slender, hipless builds. They achieved prominence as the world's eighth natural wonders. Little did we lesser physiognomies surmise they didn't look like that without the cosmetic wizardry, lighting, and team of stylists on retainer. Even as a wunderkind in the works, Oprah bowed before magnificent Colleen.

My mother willed for us a more systematic teenhood than her battle worn generation sacrificed in factories, trenches, and other war room mise en scène.

If Alison Lurie defined fashion as "the language of clothes," my closet was a polyglot—a parade of Mexican wedding gowns, African dashikis, East Indian maxis, and Bible Belt Depression-era bandits. Self-taught costume designer Theadora Van Runkle's *Bonnie and Clyde* style glamorized petty crime and pinstripes. These garments could have had a camp label sewn into their collars that read Boho-Know-How, a middle class meets migrant worker line that radiated insouciance and a personal statement that repudiated sexuality.

"Cover up, cover up," my prudish father repeated as I crossed to the toilet in a not particularly diaphanous nightgown. Undercover agent Sydney solved the mystery of his disappearing chinos when he caught Diavola rifling through his valet closet.

My Third Worldwear constituted dressing against the rampant libertine times. Unbeknownst to all family members, that Angel of Asexuality was couchsurfing under our accursed roof. (The only proviso was that this apparition didn't cause

TV static during *Mod Squad.*)

Clothes fit with a schizoid split—Hollywood or Bollywood—suburban shirt dresses or subcontinental Nehru collars. East or west, long enough to cover the subject, was always best. Outerwear masked inner psychic wear.

Classic rock consumed my consciousness as schoolwork never would. Heading up or down Belmont Hill, tenacious credenzas careened into my temporal lobe as indefatigable earworms. Concord Avenue was playing second fiddle. The Stones' *Sympathy for the Devil,* with its alternating solos, vied in my beleaguered brain box, entreating allegiance. Were the bricks really shaking on Madison Square Garden as the world's greatest band imploded on that first of two nights? November 27, Jimi Hendrix sat in the audience for his 26th and ultimate birthday. Icon Hendrix ("the most influential guitarist of all time") and supernova Taylor, two prodigies soaring above fanfare or flattery, both jettisoning the serpent of fame, catapulting them as legends incarnate.

How much better I could remember their riffs than my ABC's. Thirty airings on AM radio, touching my heart strings, but really, how pragmatic were most lessons? A hellion erased the faces depicted in illustrations in my used copy of the textbook, *Anfang und Fortschritt: An Introduction to German.* My sentiments exactly. Contemptuous of my French study guide as to when I would ever utter, "A whale unleashed a cloud of excrement." (Une baleine a lâché un nuage d'excréments.) except perhaps when conferring with much touted oceanographer Jacques Cousteau on *The Undersea World...*?

Florid and forbidding, Mrs. Khoury knew her pentameters and Elizabethan Era pop culture. During Shakespeare class, my pinkie rose pusillanimously, my throat experienced a drought. "What is a bung hole?" I dithered. Wide azure-eyed, she Cheshire Catted a simper, "An anus." The Bard's 39 plays, 154 sonnets, and sundry verses and poems, the legacy of the world's greatest writer and dramatist, summarily subordinated to the digestive tract's terminus. And linguistically, how one never willfully wants to be remembered.

Rock and roll tunes conjured cartoonish plots in rhythm and blues back beats. Indited madcap escapades (Stones' *Live with Me*), woozy euphoria (Cream's *Sunshine of Your Love*), or pure spun fantasy (Traffic's *Medicated Goo*). Our subjective visualizations of *Polythene Pam*, *Black Magic Woman*, or any of the myriad of personages dance like sugar plum fairies in our subconscious minds.

The freewheeling may pantomime superstars, too. Clothes designer, Tommy Hilfiger, forded his whole empire on that premise (American Masters' *The Boomer List,* 2014). He couldn't play an instrument or sing, but he wanted to look like a rock star. He pandered to our guilty pleasure in impersonating lead vocalists.

San Miguel de Allende, Mexico, assured a summer of school, artistry, and fabulism approximating a movie studio's recreation of a mythical town. Prepping for upcoming college application essays, I would upgrade my Spanish by studying *¡Diles que no me matan!* Juan Rulfo. (Tell them not to kill me.) *"Que fachas son,"* (What duds!) instructor Jose winked as I entered the well-ventilated classroom.

Checking me out. Schizoids probably take great pains to avoid it. Shrinking violets forgo flashiness to wither enmired, like their botanical twins, in recessive obscurity. My threads sent mixed signals.

I like it better when there are no people around; the homunculus inside my head thrummed. Others would fold, spindle, and mutilate me. A commonality among schizoids is their antipathy to being objectified—manhandled as unworthy of boundaries, feelings, rights, or the ability to negotiate situations. Pestilential parents who never safeguarded or esteemed them; their home life a miasma of being ignored or eclipsed. Relegated to unvalued family member status, little more than chattel.

Terrified may engender a delayed reaction time, but impaired isn't obtuse. Of *The Addams Family*: "They treated you like you didn't have a brain in your head," clinician Selma Landisberg deduced. As for the rest of the world: "Maybe they thought you were stupid? They didn't understand your emotional state. The whole problem is social," she then granted.

"People with SPD view others as threats, prone to abusing, manipulating, overwhelming, and enslaving." (Arthur Anders, "21st Century Schizoid Man," *Quora,* April 18, 2022.)

Me vs. them became my doomed course of action. To this one, adding another one, equaled danger. "Because they'll hurt you," Ms. Landisberg resonated. Even the outwardly beneficient would ultimately maim. Skirt teeming crowds altogether.

Omnipresent humankind would annihilate me in its ferocious, ill-willed vortex. Beware, beware, beware. Better to float as a bubble boy or girl hermetically sealed from impending menace.

Such a motherlode of rejection, starting with my mother's unloading, brought about this conditioned response. Born of the nuclear family afterward promulgated in the playground, by pubescence, a lone wolf driven from the pack, subsequently; an escape artist unchained in high school, later a hidden Houdini.

Anticipatory anxiety became second nature. I could no longer interact with others without relying on the safety hatch of my vibrant internal world. "It has always been this way," my disheartened father pooh-poohed.

Nonetheless I would dwell amicably with a Mexican family as the program assigned us to live with gracious hosts and mine truly vivified the *Mi casa es su casa* credo. After a few lame attempts to chew the fat and bungling one conversation lead upon another at dinner, I relied on chewing rather than chatting.

The foursquare dining room featured a full-sized refrigerator and TV. The latter took a considerable load off my pidgin Spanish. Electronics, the perfect tonic for 46 Country Club Lane.

Guanajuato was a gas. Heaping platters of *frijoles* (refried beans), *Jumpin' Jack Flashed* our room. I mellowed out when my roommate absented and released my Inner Ugly American Child, a furtive wellspring of caperings and imaginings. Fancy-free, I expulsed madcap laughs at Sheepdog's shaggy-dog stories.

Diavola resented our parents' surprise visit last summer. Gertrude and Sydney obtruded upon Windsor Mountain International Summer Camp. Waving and bellowing, they spied their youngest. Their brio unbounded, they lollygagged heedless of near entanglement in volleyball netting. The fast crowd smirked and grimaced at their ineptitude, razzing their loud colors and bulging flab, simply unfab, leisure wear.

On their second honeymoon here? Unglazed '40's Tonala red clay cups, bowls, and saucers with names hand-painted in white emigrated north on their wedding trip. Perhaps the pottery sustained their time together better than they did.

Mexicali *Mashuga Nuts*, my far-fetched remake of Stanley Kramer's *Guess Who's Coming to Dinner*, cast the Bermuda shorts accoutred gatecrashing couple succumbing to near apoplexy at the sight of so many unctuous dinner offerings cluttering the pine table. (What these Mass. medics termed *chazerai*, Yiddish for swine feed.)

Dr. and Missus, aghast at my gadding about and gorging on the fat of the land, bequeathing a trail of wrappers and head-scratching. Their misguided adolescent, whiling away in a patioed *casita*, indulging wholeheartedly with equal parts gratification and contrition. Their waywardness was noticeably better rounded for the experience.

Saturday nights saw El Norte gringos moldering in front of the boob tube, a girl on one arm, a Budweiser on the other. San Miguelitos, on the other hand, hunkered down in its central square, El Jardin, facing the whimsical pink, sandstone *Parroquia* (parish church). *Travel and Leisure* (July 13, 2017) named this vagabond's idyll, "The Best City in the World." Old time iron benches, colonial architecture, and cobblestone streets second the plaudit. Typical artisan wares along with embroidered clothing enhance period glamour. The Mesoamerican living theater of men and women flirting in the reverse direction as they rounded the square redefined opposite sexes.

"Donde esta su cabeza?" ("Where's your head?") the decorous shopkeeper chimed as I abstractedly fingered the showy, stitched offerings.

Texan damsels in our homestay program sewed lace onto the cuffs of their flared jeans. An ill-considered Southern Belle touch that appealed to the machismo of the San Miguelitos who went out with them. This summer was an introduction to other regional Americans.

Conspicuous for their cameras and ready cash, travelers monopolized this *pueblo magico*'s streets yawning at the jewel-toned facades. They stood in wonderment at the omnipresent gaudy *calaveras* (sugar skulls). Americans constitute Mexico's *pan y mantequilla* (7.9 million in 2019), its bread and butter.

"Muy rara," mi amigo murmured in derision at my inarguable otherness. Character disorders don't camouflage nearly as seamlessly as iguanas, those slithery, endemic masters of dissimulation. All attempts to shed my skin were for naught. "It's been with you for a very long time," my father dejectedly interposed.

An ineluctable aversion tussled with my thoughts and actions. A lugubrious force field as cloying as the lurid wraiths populating Mexican windows and tiendas. I wafted both within and without my immediate circumstances as a spectator and victim of a life unspooling.

Sometimes phlegmatic schizoids are likened to shells. Self-contained and sluggish mollusks. Misapprehended as emotionally barren beings that fall through societal cracks.

Paul Simon's *I am a Rock* intuits this mindset, and if only the rest of the world didn't mind. But they do. "Now what you don't have going for you is your personality because you're different, and people will not understand," a pal's riled boyfriend aired.

My father's ritornello replayed. Words, my handmaidens, had finally double-crossed me. They cut me to the quick. Schizoid personality disorder, an early abuse/neglect paradigm, duplicates botched children saturating such barbs. The potency of deficient parenting left in its wake a stultifying fright. And the resultant escapism.

Elinor Greenberg, PhD, CGP, Gestalt Therapist, Trainer, Writer, and Author of (the Bible) *Borderline, Narcissistic, and Schizoid Adaptations: The Pursuit of Love, Admiration, or Safety,* (published September 12, 2016) detailed in "What is a Schizoid Personality Disorder?" February 19, 2017, ... "Fantasy Life: They (SPD's) often develop an elaborate fantasy life in which they can safely experience the interpersonal satisfactions that they do not get in their actual life."

"Flight...they go into another dimension. They create a fake world. They can't adapt to the real world. The number one problem with schizoids is they don't live in reality," psychoanalyst and PhD, Pascale Gousseland stressed. The Beatles' old maid, Eleanor Rigby, so synonymous with keening insulation, existed in a dream.

Mexico still casts its spell. Boston Garden, October 11, 1972. Carlota, Carlos, and I for Santana's Caravanserai Tour concert. This wiry Chicano had won over Woodstock as a guitar-wielding force of nature. Oh my God, the headliner! Carlota and I would Funky Chicken to the seething upper mezzanine. If I didn't have a date, I had a friend, at long last. My father lent his very best, latest, and greatest pair of binoculars. So acute, so lightweight, so up close and personal that even in the birdcage, we got quite an eyeful, our sinewy picker's open fly. While covering Tito Puente's *Oye Cómo Va* (Listen to how my rhythm goes), our ambidextrous showman somehow managed to achieve closure.

Chapter 8

Flipping Pillows, Flipping Out

Many children tremble at twilight. I cowered at something subliminally darker, life certainly, death definitely, and somewhere in between, the inevitable appearance of age spots. My mother also derided obesity, varicose veins, jowls, and what's that I hear above, my heavy tread pounding the stairwell? The ravages of time—anathema to her, paralysis to me. The distaff's rubrics of natural aging read like the progeria riot act. A new roster of don'ts, don't rub your eyes; you'll get wrinkles. Don't squat; you'll develop thick calves. Don't pluck a hair; ten will grow in its place.

Old wives' tales scared the bejesus out of me. Wolfing spicy foods will trigger ulcers. Swallowing gum could lodge inert in the intestines. Reading in the dark brings about irreversible vision loss.

Grades, boys, acne, social skills, and global food scarcity weren't immediate concerns; premature haggard had me in its thrall. White nights produced bluish black shadows.

Although we lived on The Hill, my sunken eyes doubled for a refugee waif's in a foster child ad. Polite society shudders at depictions of extended spindly arms, silently supplicating intervention of shielding, nourishing families.

My arms cradled my sedative, my pillow. Flipping the obverse to get to the cool side (the reverse is 20-30 degrees below your head temperature) proved little more productive than counting sheep. Schizoid somnambulism.

Pillows could be soporific. Passive plush bodied supine bedfellows. A headrest for my head case. My mother rebuffed cuddles so filching furtive caresses from this lumpy standby soothed. Evyan's White Shoulders, a floral Second World War, All American potion, permeated her pillow, salving the battle besieged. In absentia, my fingers outlined Gertrude's delible indentations. Snuggling the bouquet of lilac, jasmine, gardenia, tuberose, iris, and lily of the valley, I drifted into disassociation, reposing as a captive and fugitive in an inebriating, oneiric nosegay.

Her brother, George, designed the Eyvan showroom in Manhattan. Their White Shoulders outclassed its domestic challengers. Beckoning, cultured peach boxes, valued for their gold embossed covering, graced both our households. The packaging exemplified '60's tasteful indulgence with its fulsome scent, implicit sensuality, and suggestion of revealing evening gowns or the possibility of dishabille.

My mother knew so much about so much. Not that she collected for mere acquisition's sake, as she truly valued the craftsmanship and history of whatever she accrued. They spoke to her, these *objets d'art*. Be it Spanish damascene, Greek meerschaum, Italian gold, Asian cloisonné, Kenyan obsidian, or Mexican pottery. As my classmates observed, our house was like that of *The Addams Family*, a museum.

Whenever I reread the lofty Greek poet Constantine Cavafy's masterpiece *Ithaka* (1911), I visualize my itinerant mother. The epic recounts Ulysses' hurdles as a metaphor for life's peregrination and the lessons learned. This bounteous second verse recalls her *occhio* (Italian for eye but figuratively for taste):

> *May there be many summer mornings when,*
> *with what pleasure, what joy,*
> *you enter harbors you're seeing for the first time;*
> *may you stop at Phoenician trading stations*
> *to buy fine things,*
> *mother-of-pearl and coral, amber and ebony*
> *sensual perfume of every kind-*
> *as many sensual perfumes as you can;*
> *and may you visit many Egyptian cities*
> *to learn and go on learning from their scholars.*

How she idolized her sibling who enlisted in the Navy as she had in the Army. They were so compatible, so endeared, and completely inseparable during his visits. Their shared aesthetics and style were more congruent than that of their partners. Their spouses essayed to fill that void.

"During World War II, Gertrude was chief nurse of a team of volunteer nurses that was flown into Hiroshima, Japan a week after the Americans dropped the atomic bomb in August of 1945. Gertrude was resolved to help the Japanese civilians, and she worked tirelessly in a makeshift hospital under less than ideal conditions," niece Lisa cited. Mother was among the first group of Army Nurses permitted in Tinian Islands in the Maranas.

Diligent Gertrude packed fragile Nipponese ceramics that withstood the vagaries of the post-war voyage home to America, only to shatter in disarray in the slipshod hands of a cleaner. Radiation imbued some pieces.

Mind over body, my mother. And yet she was photographed there as a two-piece clad bathing beauty in her unrestrained youth. Gazing at her pin-up, she shines as the very model of a wartime girl.

I wondered what had happened to her exuberance over the years. Her life's disappointments and then the malignancy that took her life. "I am not long for this world," Gertrude often avowed.

Coed Lorna and I would go to Caracas, Venezuela, on a winter break. We'd have a little getaway with touristic diversions on the beaten path and a requisite side trip to Angel Falls. A sybaritic sight for sore eyes. We were at the hotel pool and noticed Gertrude's coeval, a tanned, bikinied stunner. We both thought how different she was from our mother. This fetching, uninhibited sunbather illustrated the French phrase, comfortable in her own skin.

While ensconced in my silken, Mexican *suenos* (Spanish, dreams) world, I relocated to 142 Marsh Street. My head may have remained in the clouds, but my platformed feet would be firmly planted in a sprawling '20's era Tudor Revival House. This impressive manse could have been a first cousin to her brother, George's Great Neck Estates' home, if houses were related and if all the furnishings got along during family gatherings. "You don't really live here," Jared blurted out.

Lorna recounted the hassle of the less than mile move, but vacating is always harrowing. The landscape crew snubbed Gertrude, and she didn't marshal her usual grit in countermanding their brickbats. "Eat a bagel," one disgruntled worker jibed. Ouch, but that was the least of her pain.

Like Charlie Chan, Gertrude had a "Number One Son."

Meritorious classmate Steve, assisted with the yard work and acted as her intermediary during the debilitating swan song summer. "We must cultivate our garden," Voltaire edified as the moral of Candide. Steve learned to take care of his own needs, as I never would.

The luck of the Irish, my father's two cents clanked as he tumbled onto me. Sydney cratered in a hapless attempt to replace the chandelier bulb while lurching on a rickety ladder. "And for good measure, on plastic sheeting tossed onto just polyurethaned stairs...so reckless," my mother shook her head languorously. Dad's rough and ready affronted her equanimity.

The theory of his chaos could be traced to birth. Our births. As all gratified fathers fête their infant's arrival, Sydney did so for Diavola with a stogie perched precariously at the corner of his mouth. While handing out Cohibas to his company at their stag party, he inadvertently tipped cinders onto her newborn face.

From ashes to smashes..."Racing is the only time I feel whole," James Dean expressed before his untimely Cholame, California fender bender.

According to the American Automobile Association, traffic crashes are the number one cause of death in the age group of 16–20. This statistic doesn't diminish the status symbol's bewitchment as a ticket to freedom among teenagers. (American Academy of Child and Adolescent Psychiatry, *Driving and Teens,* No. 76, Updated April 2016)

Drivers' Ed.: My back seat driver of a dad blanched, occupying the death seat to my immediate right. White-knuckled Sydney viewed me as his problemed, not reading the cues, out of touch, daughter. From my peripheral vision, I spied him touching, or rather clinging desperately to the dashboard, quite like the shipwrecked sailors on Theodore Gericault's controversial *The Raft of the Medusa.*

"You were racing on Belmont Hill and showing off," my

father yawped, looking over his bifocals. Add to his jeremiad *Born To Be Wild.*

That's how I assumed his reckless title and one that also made me a Department of Motor Vehicles' renegade. In my usual poetic frame of mind, I forgot to bring documentation when I took my permit test. Grounded even before the key would ever enter the ignition. And now not cool in driving school, either.

A license, the carte blanche of the car-centric world Robert Moses deified, finally secreted in the glove compartment. The Angel of Asexuality, my co-driver. Bombing around the neighborhood to the forbidding cacophony of horns, bumptious bumpers, and a swarming, overheating hullabaloo of AM radio and roadsters. But such beep beep overstimulation overpowered this schizoid *schlemiel.* Oncoming chassis could veer, leap lanes, and pounce on my sedan in head on depredation. As James Bond in *Goldfinger,* I would ejector seat myself and teleport to that cushy, girly bed and awaiting Mick scrapbook.

Racing or grounded, I would never feel whole. A schizoid form of asleep at the wheel promised few willing passengers. Idling impassively in an intersection, looking a thousand ways, a choleric candidate for road rage and aggressive driving anger management classes disputed my legitimacy. "Where'd ya get it, Sears Roebuck?" he bloviated. I was on autopilot, but he didn't have a clue.

Sorrels could have been the first family of Sears. As "Where America Shops" is where we became preferred customers. Microwaves, calculators, and answering machines. Sydney's newly acquired vacuum food preserver, Seal-a-Meal, coaxed my overjoyed father to broadcast, "It's a step forward!"

The Machine Age conflated art and design earlier in the century, only to reincarnate later as the Household Machine Age. Earth Day 1970 served as the harbinger of nature-themed tints. Chirpy ocher and orange contrasted with the more low-key terra firma tones of harvest gold, umber, mustard yellow, rust, and avocado populating the floors, counters, and walls of "keeping up with the Joneses" Americana. The look on the 142 Marsh Street *mishpacha* was anything but colorful.

Dad and I would stop at Sears on the way home from his office after my routine eye exam. Sydney had to see the boys at Sears Auto Center after we bid farewell to the girls at reception. My father perceived only youthful vigor in his associates, no matter their decades.

Permed and lacquered septuagenarian Esther, stickling for message log accuracy, hollered into the receiver to the letter and without contemplation, whatever callers voiced. "Those glasses make you so dizzy you feel like you're going to retch?" she boomed in front of the entire waiting room and acted as her own version of a speakerphone.

Sears was Sydney's oasis, a kind of waystation between Ball Square and Marsh Street, that permitted my father to detox from such office drama before entering the domestic fray.

Showpiece Colleen Corby, my closet accomplice, revitalized the pages of Sears Junior Bazaar. Her batwing brows and emerald eyes made frumpy double knit skirts, quilted bathrobes, or even bodysuits worth a more lingering glance. She and her fashionista clique would have presided as high school prom queens with the brawnier competing for their undeniable pizzazz.

If only I could sizzle as a poseur amid their Simplicity pattern poses. How much more preferable than my present grim reality. My days rotated like a conveyer belt of bleak, robotic, and demoralizing rituals. Gertrude's skeletal frame dwindled and brittle, her sibilant, parched voice incommunicado to the exterior world. On scraps of paper, Mom jotted my instructions for furnishing the remaining rooms. She blinked, barely hearable; cancer rendered her inexpressive. And most gut-wrenching of all, what few utterances she managed were plaintive, moribund outbursts.

Leafing through the *Sears Wish Book for the 1973 Christmas Season*, I yearned to impede time and her fate. Sworn to secrecy from her siblings and ingroup. The terrible strain and tremendous heartache were too much to bear.

Superimposing Sears reached new heights that year as the tallest building in the world. Catalogs, veritable cornucopias of goods (six hundred and five pages in 1968!), and retail fronts that supplied consumers without culpability; every aisle of its Somerville store a tempting array of ultramodern notions, burnished in their immaculate surroundings and symmetrical displays. So plebian, so Middle American, so heartland conventional. Patterns reminiscent of Audrey's Franciscan Desert Rose patterned dinnerware elevated every dish at 17 Edgemoor Road. Browsing was a peekaboo into how the other half lived and a cataclysmal reminder of how we didn't.

Carols piping, traditional ornamentation, and flattering lighting put customers in a decidedly cheerier mood. As he was checking out, Sydney splurged on a trinket, a last-minute gift for me, a scanty concession to the season. Infused with the sentiment and sensing his goodwill, I inquired about other Yuletide diversions. He twirled, nearly losing his footing. "What with your mother up there dying?" he flayed.

Dad did take Mom to the North Shore on Christmas Day for what would be the last time as she wept at *The Crystal Ship* waterfront. "I will never see Rockport again," she whimpered. Diavola and I rolled around in fisticuffs, steeped in anguish and fury. "Hit me instead," Gertrude pleaded.

Looking at her then and thinking of her now punctures an ancient, open sore. My vivacious mother was reduced to a wig, a walking stick, and the remnants of her former radiance.

She was so terrified of dying. Our indomitable matriarch was petrified. My father couldn't find the words to lull her. He was at a loss even with his own family producing torrents of tears instead. She was so completely bedridden and enfeebled, had a fire engulfed the house, she would have perished.

My father's and Diavola's pallor blanketed the back door's pane on that last Saturday night in April. "Mom died," a discomposed Sydney unburdened. Two piercing words jolted seismically as my head tottered.

"I was awakened by the unusual sound of my father crying, a deep mournful and pitiful cry...Dad did not even know she was sick. A horror of great enormity filled our house," daughter Lisa recalled George's immense sorrow.

"After hastily packing, we jumped in a car for an agonizing four hour road trip to Belmont with Dad repeatedly moaning, 'I didn't know. I didn't know.' His sister, the person he felt closest to in life did not share her suffering and my father became guilt ridden for not having saved the greatest hero he's ever known," she averred.

"Because the atomic bomb was the first of its kind, no one really understood its magnitude or lethal extent. Gertrude was exposed to lingering radiation in the atmosphere and she died a horrific, tragic death from radiation poisoning after healing thousands of patients in Japan," niece Lisa informed.

Shell-shocked, my cousins arrived. "My own grief took a back seat to my father's. My sisters and I said absolutely nothing during the hours-long journey. We could hardly absorb my father's unrestrained grief," Lisa professed.

If the Hand of Fate gave me the finger at five, at seventeen, all ten clamped as an entire fist whammed me. Gertrude's life ended and left mine irrevocably shattered. "It will be especially hard on her," she had prophesied to my father.

"When you have something like the death of a parent as a child, everything else feels like a speed bump," Comedienne/talk show hostess, Rosie O'Donnell (American Masters' *The Boomer List*) reflected.

Sydney called to notify Lorna at graduate school in New

York, but she was out when her roommate answered.

"Tell her that her mother died." (This loutish move impelled a William Alanson White Institute staffer to question, "Is your stepmother gauche like your father?")

After a quarter of a century of marriage, my discombobulated dad in a trance doubted whether she loved him. "More than you know," I blubbered, unsure.

My bedroom was somewhat larger than a closet but substantially smaller than the others and could have been the maid's quarters. Now it would feel even more constricted as the body count rose.

In a last-ditch effort to console me, Sydney's paunch overtook my twin bed. When his shift ended, my even more *zaftig* aunt filled in. Throughout the seven days of *shiva*, she pinioned me to the mattress, leaving me like death itself warmed over.

"Sleeping in Gertrude's home was oppressive. There were reminders of her everywhere. I stared at Gertrude's beautifully painted portrait on the wall and pondered how she would want me to cope, as I was emotionally spiraling into free fall panic. Could the world that Gertrude built, with her sense of morality and perspectives, survive without Gertrude? I wasn't sure. It would take me a lifetime to make sense of Gertrude's suffering and death. I have concluded there is no sense to it. There is no sense to much of what happens in life. We just have to accept and cope," Lisa deduced.

"Cookie, you have to be strong," Aunt "Ri" urged. So would she, ditto and doubly so, for George's sake and their daughters'.

My family splintered even more adrift. My sisters fled to other locales. My father fled to a new life. That hazy, heavy summer agonized me all the more mightily, as Gertrude had predicted. My isolation and despair aggravated.

No self-help book could ease my heart. My father's

vigorous injunction to "Buck up!" or reproof, "You live in the past." resonated as all the more polarizing. My fallow mind and his (in my opinion) shallow mind never met under this roof.

South of the 38th Parallel and 142 Marsh St. intersected. Twenty years had slipped by since Sydney served as an Army Captain in Korea. Relying on his prior training, he implemented a novel course of action. "Even though we all hate one another," he admitted.

Sydney commanded his daughters to cohere, defying our usual wending separate ways. Disobey at your own risk. And those, dear reader, were our marching orders.

The Belmont High School fair weathers took an indefinite rain check from me. The sands of Revere Beach stuck to them more than they stuck to my wet blanket. The Beatles' *She's So Heavy* was my sustained mood minus the "I want you" refrain. No upside to this dark side. My childhood pals, Jared and Elvin, remained true even during my blue period. Still raw widow, Ruth Posin felt responsible for me. Gertrude's closest friends, Shirley, Evelyn, and Bernice, invited Sydney and me for dinners, intimating their sorriness through sobs and sighs. "My mother was so fond of her (Gertrude) and so missed her after she died," Bernice's daughter, Alissa (Karen), divulged.

Cheated on the last chance to confess their solidarity with my enigmatic mother, her Sisterhood continued exalting her unequivocally.

As for my father, when I most needed him, he was the least available, but then the seeds of familial destruction had long been sown.

Chapter 10

Gillett Gets A Close Shave

Seals and Crofts' *Diamond Girl,* with its lilting affirmation of coupling, aired desultorily on AM radio. A blush of love, unapologetically sentimental melody lyricizing a besotted boyfriend's devotion to his jewel of a girlfriend. The splash of saccharine I needed to assuage my dysphoria during this lachrymose summer.

Easy listening and no likelihood of a schizoid inamorata. After all, this precious paramour and her smitten lover actualize what all romantics desire and merge identities. Diamonds, the conventional symbol of fidelity and staunch union between the betrothed, endure. The world's most popular gemstone is also earth's hardest carbon, and relatively rare.

Relatively rare, too, is schizoid personality disorder. According to Andrew Skodol, MD, University of Arizona Medicine *(Merck Manual)*, SPD occurs in "about 3.1 to 4.9 percent of the general U.S. population. It is slightly more common among men. Schizoid personality disorder may be common among people with a family history of schizophrenia or schizotypal personality disorder."

Yet Elinor Greenberg would counter, "You can develop Schizoid Personality Disorder without any family history of this disorder or of Schizophrenia. However, you cannot develop Schizoid Personality Disorder as an adult." ("Can I develop schizoid personality disorder if I don't have any family history of this disorder or schizophrenia?," Quora, August 25, 2018.)

A mother may be more likely to affiliate with a same-sex offspring or female baby, accounting for the lesser risk of SPD among women. My strong resemblance to Gertrude, or in the opinion of some, spitting image, may explain her targeting me more vociferously than her other two daughters. "You got the brunt of her," a confidant disclosed.

Belmont High School had a special honorarium in store for me: its own variant of Rowan and Martin's *(Laugh-in's)* ribald comedy show award, "The Flying Fickle Finger of Fate" (a coy reference to the Romans' *digitus impudicus*—"the shameless, indecent, or offensive finger.") My classmates recognized, if not rejoiced in, my quiddity—be it an aberration, adaptation, disorder, illness, or what they called in the old country, *mishegas.* Payback time, I suppose. Approaching adulthood, I constituted a living exhibition, a P.T. Barnum's American Museum of Oddities' fixture without the admission fee.

Nonplussed, I tried to toast that cavalier time, my way. No prom, no private graduation party, no flimflam. After four years, this saturnine schiz of a senior celebrated logging far more zzz's than A's, majoring in Mick and minoring in William F.

And now add to my string of credits, gal about town, driving the blue Dodge Dart Swinger to the cafeteria, in a red plaid pantsuit and sporting specs to keep the testosterone turbocharged at bay (borrowing a page from Dorothy Parker's *"men seldom make passes."* ...epigram). I found myself the unassuming recipient of an unexpected tribute, "Most Unique – Female." (The token person of color in my year, Haitian Claude Oiseau, was the other honoree). With the "Flying Fickle Finger of Fate" vulgarity, my classmates stuck it to me once again.

My mother's presence and absence perfused the homestead. Gertrude's spirit filtered through its fourteen rooms. Her expressive eyes stared wistfully in the salon, a reminder of happier times in Rocky Neck and not so very long ago. A fledgling artist captured her allure in oils, unmindful of how much his rendition would eternize her. Oriental masks emoted in silence from the walls, all now more evocative of tragedy than comedy. And fitful nights, I cradled her pillow for solace as it was still redolent of White Shoulders.

As teens, we needed more guardianship and meal preparation than my physician father could single-handedly furnish. Sydney hired one of his patients to become our live-in caretaker. Howdy, Dotty, a Somervillian *Salt of the Earth/ Earth Mother* recombinant that nannied all children as her own.

Dotty and I presented a study in contrast, as she was as outgoing as I was withdrawn. She reposed in Cinderella's lair in reverse, relegated to the attic or rumpus room under the eaves on the third floor. Heat rises, and accordingly, so did Dotty's frustrations living in stagnant quarantine in woodsy, out of the way Belmont Hill. But bless this crusty, big-hearted woman who genuinely felt for us, but also felt a tad stir crazy. Marooned in the boonies with few distractions besides TV, Mother Nature, and us, this amiable biddy did what she could to love us back to life.

Then one lucent day, an ectoplasmic Shirley appeared at the door in her balmy whites. Seeking Sydney, she churned a cumulus of dust motes instead. How many weeks she had postponed, ambivalent about facing the finality. Shirley surveyed Gertrude's dream house, a quintessence of concrete, stucco, and status in the self-proclaimed "Town of Homes." Since spring, this prominent, wish fulfillment manse was immersed in dolor. An empty shell of a behemoth that engulfed both partners, both friends.

Crestfallen and still struggling for composure, she fingered the hem of her form-fitting shift. Shirley stared hard at the doorbell, vacillating. Her pupils fell on a rag, then a meaty hand. A hausfrau's fleshy pincers motioned her inside.

"Doc has three nice daughters, but he doesn't spend much time with them," Dotty harrumphed as she turned her attention to the wood grain Formica.

"He's a big denier...really good and really..." Shirley's voice trailed off. The mourner regretted disclosing so much so soon to this newcomer. The earthy caregiver was grateful for any company, even a griever's.

The unremitting isolation squelched our homemaker as she came to typify her namesake, going dotty, cohabiting with the aggrieved in Lonesome Locaville.

Sopping tears stained my woebegone peasant blouses while volunteering at the Mexican shop, *La Tienda*, in Lexington Center. The boutique's paltry patronage allowed me to sublimate my melancholia. Mother's Sisterhood reproved my father's desertion tacitly and offered inclusion.

Bernice's benevolent eldest, Alaina, sprung for Bunuel's *Tristana* at the Brattle as we snacked on tangerines, not the bonbons I coveted. Elvin tried to lighten my mood when we daytripped to the Madras Shop in Rockport. Gertrude's elegiac words at that scenic magnet on her final visit seared my heart as my eyes shunned the ocean.

Escort Jesse and his best buddy, John, were steadfast and regular dinner companions at the nearby HoJo's as summer subsided into meaningless minutes, motions, then months.

Jesse, equal parts enlarged brain and heart, was my rock during this labile time. Languid Victorian women inhaled the smelling salts constables supplied. Gloomy boomy, I sniffed a jar of my swain's signature Mennen cream deodorant to revive. (I wondered whether *Diamond Girl* also had such a gem in her life besides the flashy sparkler that would eventually adorn her ring finger?) Ever maternal, Mrs. Posin treated me as one of her own, even offering her greatest treasure and emollient, her secret recipe for sweet and sour chicken.

"On the day your mother died, people went to work and babies were born," my father prodded. I would be heading to Mount Holyoke College, which legendary muse and suppositional schizoid Emily Dickinson attended for a year.

My first ever 142 Marsh gardening attempted a continuation of Gertrude's pastime and as a way of fostering her memory. "Like old times," Beehive categorized my efforts.

"I think you are missing your mother," Prague Spring chirped as she steered toward Mahoney's Rocky Ledge Farm and Nursery, where we hoisted the just arrived lush, roseate, hanging begonias.

"You really didn't know him," she then added about my father. Certainly not the ne'er-do-well, deficient in the dad gene The Temptations belted out in *Papa Was a Rolling Stone,* but a victim of his era's conventional expectations and maternal demands. My papa probably didn't innately want the trappings of family. Nowadays, more social options exist, and heterosexual men may remain single longer or lifelong without the veiled suspicion of homosexuality. Tying the knot still extends respectability, especially to physicians, the most prestigious of professions. Not being committed to a marriage preempts being entrapped in a failing one and the increased odds of children *manqué*.

The wag who jested, "Mental illness is hereditary, you get it from your children." must have read Sydney's mind.

"You're driving me crazy," my father groaned from behind his Nashawtuc Country Club menu.

You are crazy, I thought to myself, as most teens would especially, those of my generation, inured to distrust those over thirty.

Concord ennobled the presumptive harmony between the colonists and the Pennacook tribe. No accord between us that day, the "same old riddle" of *We Can Talk*. Seated in a stifling sun parlor, we shared a queasy Sunday brunch, having both everything and nothing to say to one another. We could just as easily have been Rear Admiral George Stephen Morrison and his bellicose Lizard King son passing the salt in silence at the mess deck aboard the USS Bon Homme Richard. He didn't get him, either:

"...Give up any idea of singing or any connection with a music group because of what I consider to be a complete lack of talent in this direction," wrote his father, the Commander of the United States Naval Forces overseeing the Gulf of Tonkin incident.

"Forget the literary thing...," my father, the high-ranking Army Captain, interjected, "...although it's always beautifully written." The military provided its officers with servants. Nonetheless, during his tour of duty, Sydney befriended a Korean orphan loitering on the base. "All you'll learn here is foul language," he upbraided, subsidizing his schooling.

I suddenly felt ignominy underdressed in faded brown jeans seated amid the well-tailored diners. Their displeased eyes locked on me as I approached the heaping hot trays, buffet servers, and beckoning aromas. At least my appetite didn't falter.

The chipper waitress broke the wall of silence when she flaunted her spoon ring. In the '60s the silverware bands came into vogue both as precious and preserving baubles.

A father and daughter gripped their spoons in hearty readiness for the ice cream medley, now more of a melting Alaska. As the hostess placed their bowls, the coiled utensil on her lissome digit flashed in the summer sun. Almost coquettishly, she bragged that the etched floral piece had been her mother's. Sentiment adorned her finger as it had so many others for centuries before. Silver reconfigured as stories, memories, and significant occasions in the hearts and on the tapers of generations of wearers. The tradition began when 17th-century English servants pilfered their masters' cutlery to forge wedding alliances.

I wished to steal away to wherever I could heal. If only she had waved a magic wand instead.

Audrey, Elvin, Jared, Jesse, John, and Steve, an alternating, wide-eyed merry-go-round and supporting cast, buoyed my sagging spirits. The defectors, and you know who you are, acted as if I lent them money. *Easy To Be Hard.* My coterie kept contracting with the loss of my mother, my father, my sisters, and now most of my high school entourage. All gone in only four months. And soon, I would be going, too.

Watergate was the big story, and mine was yesterday's papers to my Belmont circle.

Spanish and German classes offered some daytime structure. A weekend trip with Jesse to Tanglewood and nugatory attempts to snooze in the Dart was memorable more for its contortions than its classical concerts. The Angel of Asexuality, our chaperone, occupied the mother-in-law's seat.

Steady consumption of Switzer's black licorice and frowsy three for five dollar smocks signaled my despondency. Then one fine day, the phone on the second floor trilled. *Mirabile dictu.*

A clipped, upper class voice at the other end enunciated in measured formality if she may speak to me. Flustered and several rooms from my palliative stash of Mennen's, I presumed it was the isolation ward at McLean's Hospital finally making good on all my mother's commitment threats. No, it was another exalted establishment on the line:

"You're an irregular student, but you can do it."

The dulcet tones of an emissary from an Admissions Office offering me a place in the upcoming class. Smith College on the wire, THAT girls' school and still ranked (Princeton Review) as "an incredibly prestigious, diverse, academically rigorous, socially liberal, and well-respected..." um, "institution."

Swooning, five words levitated: They must be cash strapped. Walking on air, wondering what Gertrude would want, but with Jesse's mom an alum, the die was cast. I graciously accepted my consolation prize and the chance to study with those gleaming Diamond Girls. Even though I made the cut, I construed the call as scraping the bottom of the barrel, making me a recipient of an Esquire Magazine-style Dubious Achievement Award, a displaced person among desirables.

Did I hear that correctly? My bereft eyes must also be playing tricks. Was it a desert mirage or a bearded Jim Morrison in his "Blue Lady" Mustang in a blaze (The Doors' *L.A. Woman* on Vimeo)? My blue lady steered me through my daze. "The Dodge Boys," those "good guys in white hats," pivoted us toward Star Market on Mount Auburn Street to go on a spree at Hit or Miss, a regular haunt. On this visit, the flaxen shopgirl noticed I was visibly more haunted. "You're devastated," Jack Nigle, Gertrude's erstwhile landscaper, let loose at the register at Winters' Hardware.

Audrey, Old English for Noble Strength, showed without hesitancy to be that and much more. She offered homespun succor, "You know, when you grin your whole face lights up... so much like your mother's." The Angel of Asexuality passed.

"Maybe it's too much for your father to be around you."

We were sprawled indolently on my bedspread. Our ponytails twisted in dank curlicues as we luxuriated in its sheen. Mugginess beaded the filmy paisleys that clenched our dampening shoulders. The last gasp of summer freeze framed us drooped over static headshots, "Many thought you were a really special person," Audrey reassured, combing the yearbook. Not the typical girl next door in any event.

Special has the duality of negative and positive interpretations. American Bandstand's ageless host Dick Clark reckoned that melodies conjure past remembrances, suggesting that "Music is the soundtrack of your life." The Doors' *People are Strange* could have been my tribute song.

"You're strange but nice," a drum majorette annotated in my copy.

"You're an unusual, strange kid," the mayo maven moralized.

"You are one of the all-time crazy's (*sic*)—but lovable," "*Reflections*' Editor-in-Chief," erred.

"I've always considered you an interesting and unique person. I only regret that we never sat down and had a really good talk. Without you, this grammar course would have been unbearable. I'm sure you will be a 'success' in whatever field you choose," Dr. Robert Malenka prognosticated.

Dr. Robert Malenka, The Pritzker Professor of Psychiatry and Behavioral Sciences at Stanford University, (the Halpern-Malenka Lab!) and indisputably the most accomplished in our year, authored the last pronouncement. He could not foresee all my future talks with psychiatrists or the total unlikelihood of my ever being a conventional success. How could he?

Some fared even worse through terminal illness, suicide, and the most unthinkable, murder. Not the Belmont township that Sebastian Junger had depicted. "Most people underachieve so don't feel bad," Selma Landisberg would coddle.

"When you leave high school, your teachers will still be there," my mother used to tease. She didn't live long enough to see me leave high school.

Public school, like amber, entangles nascent personalities in a reminiscent time warp. High school reunions measure Lady Luck by how much cohorts retained their looks and attained professional, material, and familial achievement. The most charmed may be enriched with all three.

Our "unbearable" grammar class was bedimmed by decades and relegated to the soot of existential disuse. Grammar is, in effect, formalized usage.

In *The Unbearable Lightness of Being,* Milan Kundera elaborates, "Living only one life...there are no means of testing which decision is better, because there is no basis for comparison...That is why life is always like a sketch." And what if the personalities and dynamics had been drawn more favorably or hadn't been present in my household?

"Well, then you could have done extremely well," Selma Landisberg concluded. "What good does it do?"

Youth represents a fresh page, the bellwether of an uncorrupted and coruscating future. College would amplify its very first rough brush marks.

As Labor Day approached, I left brainiac Jesse to heat his own frozen Stouffer's entrées, so I could make a pilgrimage to the most Russian of Brooklyn neighborhoods, Brighton Beach. My aunt and I wended from one Old World shop to the next. We dickered with merchants, as was foreseeable, in superabundant stores plundering overflowing bins beneath harsh fluorescent lighting. A select armful of *dis here* and *dat dere* Coney Island separates at the ready to trump their humble past and matriculate with the very best of them. Some of the other surrogate mothers joined forces, so my new closet would have Colleen Corby's and Gertrude's seal of approval.

But mostly, I worried more about flunking out than being

put together because, you see, the events of the last year left me a total trainwreck. "You're not as pretty as you were before," Jared taunted, that said, life would never again be as pretty.

"Go west, young woman." to paraphrase Horace Greeley, and somehow the pre-GPS Tracker blue lady and I navigated to Gillett House in Northampton, the Pioneer Valley, in the nick of time for Convocation.

Chapter 11

"The Least Sacred of Freaks"

The imperial filigree Grécourt Gates stood facing Gillett, the nexus of burgeoning feminism and the charm of yesteryear Frederick Law Olmstead's landscape design. Alumnae Gloria Steinem and Betty Friedan still cast their long shadows, valiant foot soldiers of the Movement and, with my generation, its quixotic successors.

A hippie freshman, I got there by the hair on my legs. Parking the Dart on West St. and skedaddling for John M. Greene Hall, I made it to the assembly where President Thomas Mendenhall was about to speak. His opening address and the Glee Club's performance electrified the crowd with a rousing welcome.

The auditorium brimmed with articulate, presentable young women, the ethos of future promise. Deep within the amphitheater's recesses quivered a frosh who would never quite mesh with the rest. "You feel like an outsider most (if not all) of the time. Like everyone else is 'over there', and you are never going to be like them." (*Harley Therapy Counseling Blog, What is Schizoid Personality Disorder,* www.HarleyTherapy.co.uk).

Sophia Smith's descendants, however, wanted this consolation prize, but the demons of *Sway* wanted her all the more. Academia integrated luxuriance and learning: dormitories were ivy-clad Georgian-style houses. Fridays beckoned with a tea trolley for the study weary. Unwinding to the tinkling of keys on the grand piano and a robust fire were beyond civilized. An inviting Victorian main street and across the solemn portico, our mirror image twin, Northrop House.

Both comprised single occupancy rooms, with mine being the only C-suite (as in crazy). Aside from studies, I had fun times with girls who were comparable to me, except, of course, they weren't in the most fundamental way. We were the same with a Mt. Tom of a character discrepancy.

Without Gertrude to hold my hand or pen, I enrolled in Nora Crow Jaffe's Expository Writing course. Clueless, I didn't know what the boldfaced Syllabus at the top of the page meant. "That's why you're here," a participant ribbed. Maybe their mothers also did their homework.

We became acquainted with Gerard Manley Hopkins by analyzing his poem "The Windhover." I admire any avian that can helicopter midair for lengthy periods, that stop and smell the roses kind of positive deviant in our harried world. We were two birds of a feather. *Lost in Space* soul mates. One a predatory creature, the other more a creature of prey.

Another day we would spread our wings and create a *bon mot*! Words, my long-lost friends, rejoined the fold. My semantics renamed the furrow below the nose or, more accurately, the philtrum or medial cleft.

Poet and word progenitor, Lewis Carroll, and White Supremacist, Mrs. Hickey, parented my Jabberwock or verbal fabrication, temacepid, which sounded vaguely physiological. My text merely traced a smoker's angular, sweeping arm gesture and unintentional grazing of her facial indentation. The '70's documented nicotine addiction abating, but the cool mystique for this habit still wooed. "You've come a long way, baby...your own cigarette," cooed Virginia Slims' jaunty advertising with its sly nod to Libbers.

Personifying a lifelong low-in-with-it and high-in-nitwit tug of war, I was game for anything that would improve my standing among the smart set. Baby steps began with the Bloodhound dog brand of tobacco—Old Gold. While their motto trumpeted "Not a Cough in a Carload," inhaling these ciggies, I barked more than their mascot and became a chain chewer (like my guitar gods, Lennon and Hendrix) instead.

My purist professor, Mrs. Jaffe, and I were stalled in the blue lady in Cambridge, facing a shimmering red light as the sun splayed prisms onto the windshield.

"That's a well-trimmed hand," Nora Crow scanned the vermillion trowel-shaped nails emerging from the opposing driver's side window. We were fast acquaintances going clothes shopping together in mid-August. She took a deep drag from a Merit as we eyeballed the spillover Harvard Square crowd encircling Sidewalk Sam's latest chalking.

In spite of her coaxing me to call her Nora, she remained the more fustian Mrs. Jaffe. Her Stanford bearing, impeccable Swiftian scholarship, and Marquis Who's Who distinction, "noteworthy English language educator," cowed even though she called on me to "work to make your writing equal your intelligence" when I received my first A in college.

We drew in the uproarious streetscape overshadowing the Common, and then Mrs. Jaffe lackadaisically fingered the pharmaceutical promotional keychain stuck in the ignition. I let it slip.

My cultivated prof., asquint in the glare, lip-synching the motto on this yellow plastic disk that read, *In the PM for a BM in the AM.*

Pregnant pause. Both of us pretended that the trinket didn't exist, and I wished I didn't either.

Smith played matchmaker with Big Sister-Little Sister pairings. Mine looked like an age-enhanced Goldilocks but acted more like Glinda the Good Witch. DeeDee was and still remains a consummate nurturer who selflessly cares for many. Like me, she had lost a parent in her teens, but unlike me, she had a supportive mother and sisters on her side.

Her Holy Cross hometown boyfriend, Paul, was a frequent fixture on the floor while considerably upping the floor's frequencies. Led Zeppelin's *Thank You* thundered from their salon-like living room with its maroon Oriental rug, French Provincial furniture, abundant plants, and other hipster greenery. Paul's musical tastes allied with mine, so cranking it up was fine by me. I couldn't concentrate anyhow, so what did it matter?

But it wasn't copacetic to the Nervous Nelly next door. The free concerts nearly cost her sanity. And so Yours truly became a kind of drug runner. This slip of a girl sometimes sent me on a peacekeeping mission to buy Pepto Bismol at Serio's Pharmacy. At year's end, homie Paul would graduate with an Honorary Summa Cum Loud from Smith.

A matricentric society, houses had den mothers. Ours Sarah organized more jocund group activities such as writing poems for one another. Some were toasts, and others were roasts.

A brassy English visiting exchange student, Jenny, strained

British-American relations with a limerick to Lucinda, *whose legs are so thin only Wes could get in.* Gasps and guffaws circumnavigated the Gillett lobby.

Rubrum Lily proposed to no one in particular, "Doesn't Blair look like a French king?" Her testimonial to *Oscar Wilde's Most Cherished* seemed more befitting of a court jester than a crowned head, *a quicksilver tongue, and the least sacred of freaks.*

So there you have it, a month or so into the semester, and I had already developed a rep., a repeat rep., that is.

Students' portals piqued curiosity. Gillett was a four-and-a-half-floor composite of singles as sundry as the opening tableau vivant of Hitchcock's *Rear Window.* Peering without peeping presented a sneak peek of our shared but separate lives. One adorned her walls with sheets and framed, upscale gallery loans. Another fashioned a madame's wickery lair. An outdoorsy sophomore brought her stud, an actual stallion, to the campus' stables. The bawdy poetess also imported a stud, her lascivious University of Sussex beau ("Sensu-Al").

While I may have imagined reprising Miss Body Beautiful, my days and nights were more comparable to Miss Lonelyhearts. My roomie, the Angel of Asexuality, positioned as a reminder of parietal enforcement.

As a schizoid virgin resister during the rip-roaring Sexual Revolution, I was averse to partaking in what became familiar idle chat (perhaps the onset of our present cultural malaise, TMI, or Too Much Information).

Prurience was at an all-time high. "...Boomers began to fornicate with such abandon that rabbits were asking them to cool their jets." (*The Worst Generation: Or, how I learned to stop worrying and hate the Boomers,* by Paul Begala). Stripteasing coed Linny streaked in nature's own while locked outside Gillett's glass partitioned door. "Smith to bed, Mount

Holyoke to wed," after all.

"For many schizoids, sex is associated with exposure and expectations, which are regarded as uncomfortable anxiety evoking...Most schizoids either resort to masturbation and an occasional ONS (one night stand) instead of sex in committed relationships." (Darius Schmidt, "Suspected Schizoid," Personality Disorder, *Quora*, March 10, 2021).

"The idea of having sex is usually met with disgust. They can't imagine why anyone would want to do that. Disconnection is the preferred state." (Anita Sanz, Psychologist, February 14, 2020, "What's it like interacting with people who have been diagnosed with Schizoid Personality Disorder," Quora.com).

"That's just something you have to put up with," griped a geriatric, married colleague at my New York Power Authority temp. job. Her failing eyes fixated on her filing; her thinning white dome moved like a metronome as she set forth her permutation of D.H. Lawrence's "going to the dark gods" to spinster in the making me. "That ("doing the nasty") is the biggest waste of time!" Was she a covert card carrier?

Here and there, I had what may be referred to as a Red-Letter Day, a one-shot deal, an intermediary orchestrated, but none was ever consummated. Generally, I decline such overtures, much preferring bedside reading to pillow talk in the contentment of my own self-imposed, No man's land. Better read than (sexually) dead.

Her Ladyship would rather adopt another cat than have a boyfriend, or *Gott im Himmel*, a husband. Peer pressure and romantic comedies probably make this intractability more unnerving for schizoids who simply wish to be left alone.

Rubrum Lily introduced me to a visiting Yalie/gentleman caller. My gaze met a rock star clone and his, in turn, a forlorn wretch in footie pajamas. Dish tattled to our go-between that my Andy Warhol's *Interview Magazine and Film Comment* icebreakers manifested that I was a sad sack who didn't have a life (and would likely never become a wife).

This Byronesque threat to maidenhood offered a few unsought pointers as to what kind of woman he would be, were he in my slippers. "I would be sensual. I would sweep men off their feet," he crowed. Herself realized that Himself had it all wrong, as one doesn't opt to be sensual or cool; those are qualities others project onto another.

You're Breakin' My Heart was a different species altogether from the high school dweebs and lettermen in days of yore. I couldn't believe my peripeteia. With typical schizoid ambivalence, I didn't want *Teen Beat* cover boy to go, but wasn't sure I wanted him to stay either. The Angel tendered a chaste middle ground.

We would share the bed provided he slept at the opposite end and that everything stayed tucked away.

Kiss the date goodbye:

"I'm sorry you were born in the wrong century." (to me)

"How am I going to explain this to my Yale fratmates?" (to the four walls).

"She is going to kill herself." (to Rubrum Lily).

Yep, I finally bagged a stand-in rocker only to find myself a possible premature inductee into The 27 Club.

That Club, the vaunted afterlife cloud convention sans harps for the likes of Hendrix, Morrison, and Joplin, among others. A glorified Super Group of musicians, actors, athletes, and artists who succumbed tragically as suicide, homicide, or transportation fatalities.

Witching hour, if you will, midnight oil burning, if you won't. No-nonsense Austrian exchange student, Helga sermonized, "You're a late bird!" *Nein, ich bin neurotische*, I mulled.

Soporific mornings I declined sitting with the girl on girls ordering tuna with toast instead of the leftovers upcycled as egg strata. The best perk of the day: my own brunch routine at a retro coffee shop on Green Street where my cuppa joe and the campus aligned. You know, that comforting sliver of a hole in the wall with its vintage, metal Coca-Cola advertising, uninviting, creaking, vinyl-covered stools, and glossy, dim wooden fixtures. Something about such warm places, unprepossessing as they may be, draws me like Hitchcock to a cool blond. A Dew Drop Inn sighting was my Shroud of Turin, White Whale, or fleeting glimpse of Mick.

Just the same, getting to classes punctually, or anywhere for that matter, became more troublesome. I may have been a Smithie on paper, but in person, I was the "tramp" of the Stones' *Jigsaw Puzzle* with better clothes and hygiene. The 78 LP of my life revolved like a broken record stuck in a self-destructive groove.

We were in the vanguard of the feminist movement with its cardinal expectations to super achieve in the now deposed man's world. Careerist graduates vanquished law, business, and medicine, the old boys' querencias. At a time when most determined their life's blueprint, I blanked. In spite of my generally good academic standing, I unraveled when it came to making any decision or forming any professional goal. I flailed adrift.

"The perfect job for a person with schizoid personality disorder would be lighthouse keeper." (*American Addiction Centers*).

Flailing and failing. My first ever D in a psychology class—a gut course—was because I didn't submit an assignment. What assignment? Overwrought, I confronted the professor, Barry Leon. "You miss a lot," he spluttered but uncannily, so did he when it came to assessing me. Practice what you teach! Academia has flunked connecting the dots since scholarship has been generally dilatory in shedding light on this "adaptation" (Elinor Greenberg), "(SPD) Among the least studied with virtually no empirical investigations" (*Guilford Journals*). "See, you're not so obviously disturbed," Selma reinforced.

Increasingly more perturbed, however, was the money

man helming the household. Heaving and exhaling audibly, convulsing with the mega tuition now up the chimney, "I think the whole thing is a lack of confidence," my father beefed.

"Nobody gets too close to Blair," an Australian Religion Professor, Jean Higgins, propounded, "because they'll interfere with reading." "I'd rather read," could have been my custom quote t-shirt. She discerned the most patent symptom, but had no greater comprehension than Professor Leon, my father, or I.

In this era, former first lady Betty Ford could yak to ABC correspondent Barbara Walters about boozing in The White House. When Vice Presidential candidate Thomas Eagleton's history of depression and electroshock treatment surfaced, he resigned from George McGovern's '72 campaign after no more than eighteen days.

Mental disorders remain taboo. Insular schizoids "often feel little empathy for others, which might otherwise inhibit aggressive acts. Violence committed by schizoid individuals may be related to an unusual fantasy life." *(London Pathways Partnership, Schizoid Personality Disorder).*

A danger, or different, or more dangerous to themselves because of their perceived difference? SPD ranks among the "Cluster A" or "odd, eccentric cluster" of personality disorders for "social awkwardness and social withdrawal." (MentalHelp.net). Not the stark raving mad of Randall Patrick McMurphy, "Who's the bull goose loony here?" (*One Flew Over the Cuckoo's Nest*, Ken Kesey), but more on the order of Panamanian Carmen down the hall's evaluation, "Sorrel's unusual."

"It's like having a lisp," psychiatrist Roland Foraste emphasized cavalierly. That stammer nullified any career and marriage prospects. "They (SPD's) just get by," Selma allowed. Resulting from? "Absolutely terrible luck." she bewailed.

Medieval torture living with such relations, but listening to them provided equal torment. "Someone should stretch you out on a rack," "Third rate," "Go to sleep, you've got shit rings," "Dented forehead," the scourge disgorged, battering me further into withdrawal. Pull the misanthropic string and an eviscerating tongue would dissect her victims. "Nobody likes you here," Torquemada, Grand Inquisitor's scion, issued a the truth hurts barbarous finale. "Is she still at war with herself?" my astute Brooklyn aunt inquired. Sibling rivalry from Cain and Abel to Joan Fontaine and Olivia de Havilland and beyond catalogues full frontal *Bitch*iness whatever the age or rage.

Maybe Sartre had such odious consanguinity. "You were thrown into the ring with too many opponents. They set the stage...," Selma inferred. Mine sealed my freakish schizoid fate. "Way too much criticism. And someone not as sharp or as sensitive would not have been so damaged. I wouldn't care for people either," she concurred.

"A pretty shaky childhood. They obviously have gone through their own hell and survived it," Arthur Anders (*21st Century Schizoid Man*," Quora, August 16, 2021).

Chapter 12

That's the Way
the Top Flops

Henry Darger's life dissolved as mine evolved. If you have never heard of him, that's exactly how he'd like it. A reclusive janitor who dwelled in an unpresuming room for forty years. His main chance came on entry to a Chicago nursing home when an encouraging landlord upended his treasure trove of outsider art.

"What's the use of being talented if no one knows about it?" my father carped as I would not show my writing to anyone.

Henry Darger was a textbook schizoid, the one we all know but hardly get to know: "Henry Darger is that man living in that house on your block that you've never met....He's the man who never talks about his family, girlfriend, wife or friends and by all accounts has none." (Project MK-Ultra: Henry Darger, inaugural post of this blog, August 24, 2012).

Darger embodies schizhood sequestering right down to his custodian career. If only I had more perspicacity and pursued an isolative path while in school. Needless to say, Daddy didn't send me to Smith to become a cleaning lady.

In 1975, my alma mater's exultant "A Century of Women on Top" sloganed t-shirts made more than a fashion statement. The sassy innuendo aroused male lust and female hubris in this strivers' paradise with its splendiferous pond. Super achievement in each of life's arenas or having it all was not only expected, it was exacted. Diamond Girls Julia Child and Sylvia Plath, among others, were hard acts to follow. The Seven Sisters postulate trailblazing; schizoids leave an incidental trail for posterity.

"I expect to hear great things about you," one of my classmates, Chuck, lauded. As the years racked up and repetitive trauma arose, that approbation nagged at me like an illusory Tsetse fly embedded on the spine of a black rhinoceros. Not having the emotional state preempted fulfilling others' presumptions or my name school's destiny in whatever field. And most demoralizing, I had no control over it whatsoever. "You were bright enough to pass the courses but, of course, couldn't achieve your potential," Selma cajoled. Joel Brodsky's *Young Lion* had everything but the emotional state.

And more harakari tidings: "The chances of someone with this disorder climbing the corporate ladder are....NIL." Selma's reedy and tilting delivery underscored each dispiriting word, "I would just keep your head above water... You can't compare yourself with someone who's normal," she accentuated.

Smith and other elite academic institutions may set a bar

even too high for those with a greater likelihood of becoming outliers: "You graduate from here and think you can be queen of the world....So pervasive is this emphasis on visible success that some alums (Smith) told me that they hesitated to return (to reunions) at all or found it very difficult when they did." (*Nobody's Perfect: Alumnae Share Their Real Lives, Woes and All,* Julia McKenzie, '79).

Having it all wasn't tenable for most students. Having none of it at all was most tenable for this schizoid. I would never come into my own—not there, not here, not anywhere. Like a paranormal force constricting thoughts and actions, withdrawal strangulated my self-regard as a duplicitous, silent killer. SPD plays the heavy in this against all oddballs story.

Finding yourself and getting your act together, in addition to other hackneyed pep talks and platitudes, won't cure the defective. Imagine waking up and having to redo household chores, going around in circles for a misplaced object you are wearing (your glasses on top of your head), or becoming ensnared in a tailspin for an actual or imagined lapse. Prevailing on the footloose foghorns to *Focus!* is as ineffectual as inciting the clinically depressed to *Cheer up!*. Mind candy may help, but a lot of the time, my head quakes in dissociative drum beats. "Blair's a space general," blunt Ingrid deadpanned.

Having all of it in my carrel at Neilson Library. Having a whole stack of cumbersome textbooks, that is, most of which I would never open within the course of a weekend night. Ambitious, if extraneous, delusional flotsam and jetsam, "I would describe you as a person whose contact with reality is not always that great." Thus, sprach Selma.

Studying religion probably implied a clumsy crash course in self-healing from my mother's profound loss. My major became the proverbial albatross around my neck, the supreme rift between Sydney and me—big time.

Any liberal arts agenda has limited practical application beyond honing intellectual abilities. "She is considered one of the finest in our department," head Bruce Dahlberg confided to my father during an in-person consultation, but that never placated him.

SPD, not my curriculum, undermined my future. Most BA students transition seamlessly because their familial circumstances assure they can adapt more readily and hold jobs.

And I know what you are thinking. We all have more baggage than some airport carousels. Barring impairment, you were able to work.

According to Clinical Psychotherapist Karen Arluck, defining "The key features of schizoid personality disorders"... Did not feel they were entitled to have their own feelings or often felt they were made to conform to whatever their caregivers told them to feel or do." (*Why are schizoids so weird?, Quora.com,* May 24, 2017).

Digressing from my sisters who could form goals (architect, Latin teacher), I simply couldn't and didn't know why (they would put me in closer relation to others). Throughout this undergraduate process, I felt more puppet than pupil at an venerated college where my survival, given my gravely depleting emotional state, that I was admitted at all, handled myself fairly well, and formed a few lengthy, albeit distant friendships, was nearly miraculous.

As Elinor Greenberg recounts, "It is quite possible that some of these high functioning, intelligent, and self-reflective people might evolve out of their learned mistrust and intimacy issues as they mature, get away from their abusive family, and start thinking for themselves. It is likely that they would still have some scars and Schizoid traits, but they would no longer qualify for a diagnosis of Schizoid Personality Disorder if they develop whole object relations." (Quora.com, July 27, 2019, and *How Do You Develop Whole Object Relations as an Adult?," Psychology Today,* February 11, 2019).

Nomadic began at nineteen with moving to ultramodern Cutter House adjacent to the coffee house, The Davis Studies (Campus) Center. My straightforward Professor Emeritus of Ancient History, Louis Cohn-Haft, "An Introduction to Greco-Roman Thought," had his office next door. We often crossed paths. His lips moistened in courtly pursuit of a stacked prima donna; mine for a stack of equally well-rounded flapjacks. The Professor had choice words for my scholasticism—"breezy and slapdash" as annotated on the periphery of my midterm essay.

One, come to think of it, breezy Friday, he heaped more choice words on my exercising a woman's prerogative while changing my outfit four times during the course of the morning. I did not share Cohn-Haft's avidity for dead peoples in general and being schizoid, living peoples in particular. The Professor may have had a passing fancy in me as an ongoing case study of a campus live one. Cohn-Haft nudged me to get going with class assignments as I was remiss in taking initiative.

Whatever Gets You Thru the Night. Tossing and turning, for the most part—be that as it may, with bedwetting and spotting becoming bygones.

Halloween approached. Foliage ablaze and frost on the pumpkin marked its fanfare. Rubrum Lily invited me to a house masquerade party, and I gamely accepted. The female ululation, I have nothing to wear, echoed among closets. A frantic intonation pulsed from the Hooray for Ivy Day Quad to singular Capen House's lovey-dovey gazebo, cupola, and rear gardens, whisking the deciduous trees blithely downsizing.

As All Hallows' Eve insinuated, my wardrobe seemed regrettably hollow. A prop stylist reincarnated, I gave props to Practically Worn, the consignment shop on Green Street.

"What's that?" the curmudgeonly return librarian inquired as he spotted me near Neilson Library.

"Er...Bianca Jagger." My head bowed, eyes averted, and throat desiccated. I forgot that the Reference Library didn't house stacks of weekly *People*.

"You'll need to get a tan," his freckled brow crinkled in dubiety. No tanning beds at the time, and probably no one would guess what my scrapbook costume made flesh was anyhow. I thrifted a flouncy tiered antique petticoat—what Gertrude would have spurned as a *schmatta* (Yiddish for rag)—and felt pretty full of myself that at least one of my many Walter Mittys was fulfilled.

To Rubrum Lily, it wasn't a getup; it was a getaway from my own personhood. Wanting to be someone else surpassed dressing the part.

Other people's lives captivated me far more than my own. Tabloid and fanzine readership got me thru the night. Without factoring that the high life portrayed may have been accidental fortune or more strictly constructed through strategy and planning (neither of which I would have been able to recreate).

"Most people feel pretty good about themselves," Selma affirmed, as I certainly never did. "Shyness is a form of anger." At Smith, I became an autodidact studying featherless bipeds, my own Anthropology minor with *People* as my encyclopedia.

"There is a subset of people who are different from the normal population. Their brains are wired a bit differently, or they went through experiences in their lives that contributed to their introversion, social avoidance, and shyness. They may have been sensitive children who were neglected or abused, never encouraged to learn about the world around them. Their feelings may have been invalidated when they were young, so they learned to keep their emotions inside instead of sharing them with others around them. They learned to be self-sufficient instead of relying on others and on society for their needs. Some of these shy individuals who we classify as loners may be afflicted with a disorder called schizoid personality disorder."(J.B. Snow:*The Misunderstood Loner: An Explanation of Schizoid Personality Disorder, 2015*).

By now, *tsuris* (Yiddish for trouble) could have been my epithet.

"If you had a roommate in college, maybe you wouldn't have this disorder?" Sydney vocalized as a panged *moue* flashed across his glum features. A new norm for the dorm?

"*Schmegegge* (Yiddish for nitwit), you get involved in a lot of foolishness!" he fumed.

"Put it down, you'll break it," my father yowled a familiar chorus when I handled his property.

"They had no idea what you were talking about!" Dad denounced my obfuscation.

(*Nota bene*, we do hear compliments, maybe not often enough, "Why is a smart girl like you having so many setbacks?," "You're a survivor.")

Family Affair:

"I don't know what I did to deserve a daughter with MS and you with your mental problems," Sydney caviled, fisting the firmament like Job. "That man should be shot at sunrise," Selma howled in session. My silent partner, The Angel of Asexuality, nodded in assent.

Chapter 13

Asexual and the City

"Paris is for lovers. Maybe that's why I stayed only thirty-five minutes," Humphrey Bogart, *Sabrina*.

Chanteur Jacques Brel's musical had been adapted the prior year and made this fabled destination all the more *recherché*. The *joie de vivre* of *Alive and Well* followed me to Gillett, Cutter, and finally, Cushing set in the uppermost Great Quadrangle. One of ten Depression-era completed houses is where I would pass my junior year. Religion courses filled my curriculum, but *wanderlust* filled my cerebellum. Dang! I should have gone abroad this year when I had the chance.

My German was better than my French, but *How ya gonna keep them down on the farm now that they've seen Paree?* So I applied for the program and bided my time.

Cushing softened Cubist Cutter's rough edges while suggesting some of Gillett's good bones. The quad circumscribed a micro-neighborhood of picturesque, identical houses. Though I tried to join in the gaiety, Hilaria rightly construed that I was not a party person. To Nia's disappointment, I became noticeably more retiring when we attended one together.

Kegs funneling beer were the focal point of these bibulous, blowsy shindigs. One Yuletide revelry, in particular, would become immortalized in Smith's history for its inordinate "you had to be there" moment.

The ladylike sitting room got all Frank Capra gussied up. Couples linked, ornaments shone on fir roping, and spices seasoned a citrusy punch in a crystal bowl—all the appurtenances of a traditional, sophisto-skewed, festive-hued gala.

Sets of blotto eyes all at once shifted in the direction of one guest. Center stage, a visiting male straddled the overstuffed sofa, yanking down his pants. A manspreader who had the best seat in the house showed his appreciation with a scatological endowment to the college—a merry brown he would never live down. *Saturday Night's Alright for Fighting.*

"Whoa, if you ever want to see 80 people clear out of a room faster than a bomb scare," Mae Anne's boyfriend, Trey, embroidered every retelling. The life of the party tale took on a life of its own.

For us homebodies, the buffet, bar, or both, become home base.

"Command social performances like large family gatherings, holidays, baby showers are almost intolerable. The idea that they have to manage a college setting or a job with other people can sometimes be overwhelming and more than a little anxiety-provoking or depressing." (Anita Sanz, Psychologist, Quora.com, February 14, 2020, *What's it like interacting with people who have been diagnosed with Schizoid Personality Disorder?*)

The '70's made air travel middle class and checking more suitcases acceptable. The transatlantic flight officially began by the seat of my pants, that is, sitting on my American Tourister to force its closing. Schlepping well in excess of my own poundage in wardrobe and personal effects, I envisioned a *Champs-Élysées* conquest upon landing, not the greater likelihood of a hernia.

Such *prêt-à-porter* spoke volumes for overcompensating materially and gesturally while operating The Full Monty in inferior schizoid mode, ("Which you have no reason to feel intellectually," Selma harangued.)

Air France taxied to the terminal with one permanent pressed and distressed airsickness bag of a mademoiselle aboard. As the old chestnut goes, "If you look like your passport photo, you probably need the trip." Disembarking at Charles de Gaulle Customs, *bienvenue à un phobique fatigue* living among the *brusque* xenophobic. What the Carter was I thinking? Jetlagged in a zigzagging cab headed to what could have been a Henry Miller-style flophouse for my own version of John Lennon's "lost weekend."

I may not have triumphed on that boulevard, but McDonald's most definitely did, and their Big Mac with Béarnaise Sauce, was invincible! France, the self-appointed signpost of global civilization, had lost standing to the invading American barbarians. The vulgar, uncouth *Junk Food Junkie* Anglos, hordes of (*Quelle horreur!*) down filled parkas, and anoraks transgressing *arrondissements. (France in the 1970s: A Time of Decline, Doubt, and Anti-Americanism,* Adrien Sheppe, Americans in Paris, Fall, 2010, December 15, 2010).

The Smith *troupeau* met at the Tuileries Garden, where I recognized Cushing's Tonya and Cutter's Lorilee at the orientation. Alison and Constance from Wellesley and some from other girls' schools interspersed, but let's face it, we Seven Sisters were cut from the same cloth—Levis and overalls which telegraphed tourists.

And so the Junior Year Abroad ceremoniously commenced. Overnight its initiates seemed almost Photoshopped. If not chicer, unflappable in their pertinacity to drink in the radical change in study and culture. We imbibed the South of France, a spectacularly magnificent region, at this supernally ethereal time of year. *Aix en Provence*, the locality of our fall intensive program, where I would assimilate more Calissons then cellulite (*peau d'orange*, doesn't everything even repulsive sound so much better in this language?) than fluency. Mmm... I would have married those almond-shaped marzipan sweets with the slightest nuance of melon in each blissful bite.

"Jeunes filles, travaillez!" ("Young ladies, work!") flinty, old-school Madame Line Barret protested. Her fastidious, braided skullcap and spiffy, buttoned-down Coco Chanel style. *Soignée*, she was inscribed in the '50's, whereas I was engraved in the '60's. Maybe *l'enseignant* detected *babacool* (French slang for nonconformist) in her ten o'clock scholar, *"Mon petite amie qui est toujours en retard."* ("My little friend who is always tardy.") The well-entrenched phobia made getting anywhere punctually more problematic.

Alors, Aix marks the spot where I was studying people again and my host family, in particular. The Famille DeCormis inhabited the '40's, when *film noir* enshrined *fumeurs* (smokers). If I would leave the Land of the *Bah Écoutes* ("Land of the Well Listens") with nothing else to show for it, my lungs would. No Surgeon General in these parts harped on them to boycott those inescapable blue Gitanes boxes.

Through thick secondhand smoke and thin dialect, somehow or other, I would have to wing it when enrolled soon at the tony host university, the august Sorbonne. With God as my copilot, my grade point average would disappear in effluvium!

A *naïf* abroad, I conjured Miller's *Tropic of Cancer* inimitable French classroom and a smarmy Rip Torn-style *l'instituteur* overseeing. The actual staging, *au contraire*, was a former military site with a stern Jesuit pontificating. The University of Paris IV at Clignancourt in the 18th arrondissement—so close to Sacré-Coeur, but so far from Dieu.

I froze as the instructor's chalk-striated, creased jacket slinked through, then ambushed the captive studentry. A Gallic Grim Reaper, he worked the room nattering at an unforgiving speed.

In my chronic campus catatonia, *mes copains*, I sat too congealed to raise my hand all term. *Zut!* I would die a martyr's death rather than commit Franglais amid this cut throat pool of frogs with famously little politesse for crass, plus size Yanks butchering their language.

The Program's Directrice, Madame Delage, was *vachement* (French argot for bloody) unhinged as to how I'd manage in such a demanding academic environment. She chuckled, inhaled, then exhaled. *"Tu parles à peine francais!"* she frowned. ("You barely speak French!") Maybe a Berlitz course was in order.

As for housing, I would put in for a widow. Or ask *La Directrice* to peruse her Rolodex for a reasonable facsimile— that needy blabbermouth who could leech on me to her or his heart's desire.

Then applied linguistics with my choice of entertainment— erotic cinema (not much dialogue and minimal subtitles) to jumpstart matters. The Angel of Asexuality looked the other way. *Emmanuelle* was my primer, a soft-core *Alice in Wonderland*. The libertine novice had as her mentor a haberdasher's vision of a geezer (Alain Cuny as Mario) who wore crisp suits regardless of the context or Celsius.

A *Neuilly-sur-Seine* newb; I got my wish and my widow. "It is the wealthiest and most expensive suburb of Paris." (Wikipedia) Mme Martin cohabited with her two brunette, and somewhat funereal daughters, Bea and Sabine, along with their scrappy terrier. When they weren't *a la campagne* in Chartres *pendant le* weekend, they mostly convened in the stagnant living room of their mausoleum-like flat. The only vivid sign of life was the ephemeral bouquets that bedecked the coffee table. If Chez Martin humanized a paint swatch, it would have been Paris Gray.

An *Elle* and *Marie Claire* background didn't prepare me for these flesh and blood Frenchwomen. A decidedly deglamorized duo; Bea was as porcine as Sabine was equine. The lecherous Romans would have outright rejected the rape, abduction, or kidnapping of the latter.

As usual, I was quiet and kept to myself (cut-and-dried serial killer post-atrocity police blotter lingo), attending classes and scouting the local color, *Montmartre* and its *Funicular,* the *Marche aux Puces* (Flea Market), and the cabaret, *Lapin Agile* to which Picasso paid tribute in his selfsame masterwork (1905). In spite of gross social anxiety and even grosser savaging of the native tongue, I made do with a certain *je ne sais quoi.* (I don't know what.)

My itinerary departed from the standard Michelin Green Guide. A pilgrimage to the grave of Mr. Mojo Risin' (an anagram of the unscrambled spelling of Jim Morrison) in *Père Lachaise* was on the top of my bucket list.

Jimbo slugged 36 beers during his final recording session, too soused to stand for the album cover. Half dead, he departed the City of Angels destined to be gone in three months. William Blake penned the sententious, *The road of excess leads to the palace of wisdom.* This trashed path led to an overflowing eyesore of beer cans, cigarette butts, "photos, flowers, notes, ribbons, and candles" (*Paris Cemetery on moving Morrison grave: no way* Maya Vidon and Jon Dyer, *USA Today,* July 27, 2016), buffeting a bronze bas relief tombstone.

Rear Admiral George Stephen Morrison's commemoration of his prodigal, named after General Douglas MacArthur, with its elegant display of paternal love, obscured the squalor and sorry circumstances of their squabble. "My son had a unique genius, which he expressed without compromise," he relented a decade after his demise. His "music for the different," my long-term "special friend," helped me reconcile the limitations of both our patriarchs.

By spring, the storybook *merveille* of April in Paris wasn't merely The Count Basie Orchestra's sheet music (*April in Paris*). My grades, while not *formidable,* attested *"Pas mal de tout,"* ("Not bad at all!") Mme Delage. As they say in French, *"Le jury était sortie."* Language command: *"Tu a fais un progrès fantastique,"* Bea. Social skills: *"Il y n'a pas de méchanceté; vous êtes une inquiète,"* *"Sa mère,* Madame Martin." ("No malevolence, you're a worrywart."). Junior Year had a senior moment now and again with a schizoid walk-on. "C'est pas pour passer dans une chambre!" ("It's not for staying in your room!") Bea contended.

Belmont buddy, Elvin, and I would meet and explore Europe that summer. Wrench your mind to a time when communication was by air mail and international calling was a luxury. We missed one another, and I found myself solo with a Eurail pass. Of course, being alone was second nature, and most spoke English, so I was generally an at ease *flâneuse.*

A package tour would never have provided some of the most disarming remembrances. Chantilly, on the outskirts of Paris, is best known for its whipped cream and its *Château.* Late one summer afternoon, I arrived at the latter only to find its wilted guard catnapping. The ornate doors of this architectural confection would soon shut against the *chaleur* (heat).

This sole functionary could not leave his post to guide. Through heavy lids, he saw my expression slacken. And with the laxity of a father loaning his car keys for a first date, he handed the set to me. Who says chivalry is dead?

I hastily checked my takeout chicken container in the

mirrored vestibule and felt supremely royal, admiring the gilt-edged finery of each capacious, Rococo ormolu room. Unfortunately, I inattentively left a going away present. My traveling companion's breast and thighs spent the remainder of the weekend locked inside.

Neuro in Euro's holiday was the usual catalog of must-see capitals. Between rough and tumble hostel nights and budget-minded *cafés*, the fluttering postcards of stupendous sights flickered almost cinematically past the train window.

Returning to Paris, I was set on visiting two feminists with the most far-reaching effect on my stay. Gustave Eiffel's tower, nicknamed, *La Dame de Fer* (The Iron Lady), has stood over many marriage proposals and stood in for Citroën as a vertical billboard. Her hulking shadow lurked everywhere with the reassurance that having a crazy design (like my own) can become respectable anon.

Not everyone paid homage to this imposing harridan, the City of Light's fanciful symbol. France's superlative short story writer, Guy de Maupassant, ate lunch daily in her restaurant because it was the only place in town where he could not view that multistory monstrosity above. In *Bah Écoute, restaurer* is to restore and what any praiseworthy eatery should do, *finalement*.

As might be expected, I also wanted to pay my respects to the iron-willed Madame Delage and thank her for all she had done for (*"dans sa reve,"* in her dream) me and the rest of the crop. I related my travel adventures around the Continent and the Aegean, but this time, she tee-heed and exhaled, smiling, "Your French was not the *ne plus ultra* (the very best) of the group's, but you improved the most. You were *tout simplement*, the most determined."

"What are you thinking of doing when you return to the States?" she asked diplomatically.

Naturellement, I drew a complete blank. *La Directrice*

pressed a clope to her ready lips. "*Bah écoute,* you could have a rather hard time in graduate school," she scowled. My *bête noire,* withdrawal, that vile interloper, nipping at my heel?

"You have a way of looking at things that's uncommon, you're original..." pent shoulders she suspired, "but *cela ouf... un problème!*" Trials and tribulations I most certainly would have, but Madame Delage, like most others would not know the half of it.

Still again, Psychologist Anita Sanz saw the upside of this dark side: "I have a great deal of respect for people with this disorder (SPD), as I feel great compassion for their struggle to be understood and respected when they are so different from other people. The very thing that makes most people feel human is the thing that they lack: the desire to bond and connect. To feel so different and to be so different in this world is an incredible challenge. They have amazing insight into the ridiculous foibles of us 'feeling' types, though, and I have learned so much from the clients I have worked with. They are intelligent, creative, and almost every one is an amazing artist, writer, or poet, and lover of animals." (*What's it like interacting with people who have been diagnosed with Schizoid Personality Disorder,* Quora.com, February 14, 2020).

"Well, you saw what it's (Schizoid Personality Disorder) like to live with," another therapist sputtered.

I did. Now make that a merciful bullet in the back of my head in my sleep.

Seated for dinner at Bread and Roses' soup kitchen (yes, you read that right), The Unabomber's *doppelgänger* slumped diagonally across from me. An untrammeled beard, a coffee-saturated, rumpled shirt, a fixed gape into infinitude, and a faint voice that nary spoke. Staffers would have gladly offered clean, even new clothing had he asked. But of course, my compadre wouldn't.

A zomboid, leading man in our Lifestyles of the Poor and

Anonymous. We may seem little more than glassy-eyed characters with thousand-yard stares stumbling and bumbling underfoot. Fodder for supercilious Type As to snap their fingers then snort, "Are you retarded?"

But first, let me offer our collective apologies for the involuntary hurt and inconvenience we cause.

Recall Dr. Winston O'Boogie's serenade to the lovelorn or call for caritas. Schiz Kidz have a greater propensity for schizotypal personality disorder or schizophrenia. That psychosis is all the bleaker as: "They don't live very long. They don't take care of themselves, and they're not treated very well by other people," a social worker resigned, unaware of my DSM credential.

When you finish this chapter, please leave with more compassion. No day is our day.

Charity begins at home. Thwart SPD among your own, if at all possible. What happened to me could happen to them or anyone.

"It is a set of attitudes and coping mechanisms that begin in early childhood." (Elinor Greenberg, Quora, August 25, 2018, *Can I develop schizoid personality disorder if I don't have a family history of this disorder or schizophrenia?*)

This memoir is a caveat, and its late-life debut a testament to how tenacious this imprint is. To resort to clichedom, you reap what you sow. A word to the wise— be wiser with your words.

And to you, my fellow schizoids, my parting words: Have no fear; they're just *People*.

Our odyssey constrained marching to the beat of a different drummer, but schizoid lives should distinguish not extinguish a contrarian flame:

As you set out for Ithaka, I hope your road is a long one, full
of adventure, full of discovery.

Laistrygonians, Cyclops, angry Poseidon—don't be afraid of
them:

You'll never find things like that on your way
as long as you keep your thoughts raised high,
as long as a rare excitement
stirs your spirit and your body.
Laistrygonians, Cyclops,
wild Poseidon - you won't encounter them
unless you bring them along inside your soul
unless your soul sets them up in front of you.

Ithaka by C.P. Cavafy

EPILOGUE

"Of course I'm respectable, I'm old. Politicians, ugly buildings, and whores all get respectable if they last long enough.

- Noah Cross, *Chinatown* (1974)

POSTSCRIPT

A dreamy playlist of "SPECIAL FRIENDS" in order of appearance.

Vic Mizzy, "The Addams Family Theme"
Alan Jay Lerner and Frederick Loewe, "Camelot Musical"
Cream, "Born Under A Bad Sign"
Mary Hopkin, "Those Were the Days"
Harry Warren and Johnny Mercer, "Jeepers Creepers"
Judy Garland, "Judy at Carnegie Hall"
Aaron Neville, "Tell It Like It Is"
Charles Strouse and Lee Adams, "Bye Bye Birdie"
The Beatles, "She Loves You"
The Beatles, "All My Loving"
The Beatles, "Till There Was You"
The Beatles, "I Saw Her Standing There"
The Beatles, "I Want to Hold Your Hand"
Mister Rogers Neighborhood, "Won't You Be My Neighbor"

The Beatles, "Nowhere Man"

The Doors, "People are Strange"

Simon and Garfunkel, "The Sound of Silence"

Beach Boys, "Good Vibrations"

The Turtles "Happy Together"

Rolling Stones, "Paint It, Black"

Scott MacKenzie, "San Francisco" (Be Sure to Wear Flowers in Your Hair)

The Beatles, "She's Leaving Home"

The Beatles, "Birthday Song"

The Doors, "When the Music's Over"

The Doors, "Love Me Two Times"

The Doors, "Light My Fire"

Sergeant Barry Sadler, "The Ballad of the Green Berets"

Country Joe and The Fish, "Feel Like I'm Fixin' to Die"

The Rolling Stones, "Sympathy for the Devil" (Live at Madison Square Garden)

Crosby, Stills, Nash and Young, "Woodstock"

The Beatles, "Let It Be"

Gerome Ragni and James Rado, "Hair the Musical"

The Doors, "Hello I Love You"

The Jimi Hendrix Experience, "Purple Haze"

The Jimi Hendrix Experience, "Foxy Lady"

Bob Dylan, "The Times They are A-Changin'"

African American Spiritual, "He's Got the Whole World in His Hands"

David Bowie, "Space Oddity"

Steve Miller Band, "Space Cowboy"

The Beatles, "Across the Universe"

The Zombies, "Time of the Season"

Perry Como, "There's No Place Like Home for the Holidays"

Jerry Vale, "Silver Bells"

The Beatles, "All You Need is Love"

Randy Newman, "Gone Dead Train" ("Performance")

Harry Nilsson, "One is the Loneliest Number"

Frank Sinatra, "Strangers in the Night"

The Rolling Stones, "Live with Me"

Cream, "Sunshine of Your Love"

Traffic, "Medicated Goo"
The Beatles, "Polythene Pam"
Santana, "Black Magic Woman"
The Rolling Stones, "Jumping Jack Flash"
Paul Simon, "I am a Rock"
The Beatles, "Eleanor Rigby"
Tito Puente, "Oye Como Va"
John Barry, Leslie Briscusse, and Anthony Newley, "Goldfinger"
The Doors, "The Crystal Ship"
Steppenwolf, "Born to be Wild"
The Beatles, "I Want You (She's So Heavy)"
Seals and Croft, "Diamond Girl"
The Rolling Stones, "Salt of the Earth"
The Band, "We Can Talk"
The Temptations, "Papa was a Rolling Stone"
Three Dog Night, "Easy To Be Hard"
The Doors, "L.A. Woman"
Rolling Stones, "Sway"
Led Zeppelin, "Thank You"
Harry Nilsson, "You're Breakin' My Heart"
The Rolling Stones, "Jigsaw Puzzle"
The Rolling Stones, "Bitch"
John Lennon, "Whatever Gets You Through the Night"
Sly and the Family Stone, "Family Affair"
Eric Blau and Mort Schumann, "Jacques Brel is Alive and Well and
    Living in Paris"
Walter Donaldson, "How Ya Gonna Keep 'Em Down on The Farm?
    (After They've Seen Paree?)"
Elton John and Bernie Taupin, "Saturday Night's Alright for
    Fighting"
Larry Groce, "Junk Food Junkie"
Count Basie and His Orchestra, "April in Paris"
Barbra Streisand, "People"

"Each one has a song...has his interpretation."
(1 Corinthians, 14-26)

Preserve your musical memories and those flashbacks on
www.RockingTributes.com. Never has the soundtrack of
your life been so simple to record.

ACKNOWLEDGMENTS

Beholden to my beloved parents, Sydney and Gertrude, for their creation act which spurred mine.

Grateful to my sisters who went along for the wild ride.

Shout out to the acclaimed author, Harry Freedman, who made mine his book of the month selection.

Profound gratitude to NFB's review editor, Eleanor Rummell, who brought Eleanor Rigby's story to life.

Adank to Leo Rosten, "The Joys of Yiddish" for translating my parents' secret code.

Bravo to the Atmosphere Press team, who, unlike some competitors, wasn't full of hot air. Special appreciation to my Cupid, Acquisition Editor, Shelley Lee, Development Editor, Tammy Letherer, Managing Editor, Alex Kale, Production Manager, Erin Larson-Burnett, Art Director, Ronaldo Alves, and Digital Director, Evan Courtright.

Special thanks to my "That's not writing, that's typing" early readers - Alissa Bixon, Audrey Broner, Kirk Citron, Joe Cunningham, Maria Del Rio, Dianne Fanelli, Roger Favale, Andrea Goguen, Steve Gruber, Karen Haley, WenWen Lin, Harold Masters, Elliot Matz, Roy McDonald, Leslie Ryan, Ed Rynne, and Joan Schwarz.

Deepest gratitude to those once-upon-a-time Glimmer Twins for their staying power:

Elliot Matz divined, "Your whole thing is your writing."

While Joel Sadagursky opined, "It would be a shame if you came and went without a book."

Kudos to my cast of clairvoyants:

Lisa and Gerard Leval, who saw a book in my future.

Crystal Brown, who saw two.

Playwright/copywriter Blake Levinson, who saw a whole series.

A big hand to the dearest departed Theresa Shelzi, who lent me her ears as my project confidante and catalyst.

To my swain, Richard Spain, who never complained.

High-five to the "From Crayons to Perfume" Belmont High School honorable mentions:

Louise Alfred

Elaine Appel

Adam Apt

Barbara Habeshian Azarik

Seth Barad

Sharon Bird

Barbara Pacl Bjornson

Audrey Broner

Kirk Citron

Cynthia Papoulias DeAngelis

Jay Ferreira

Bill Gnerre

Donna Madanjian Griswold

Karen Johansen Haley and
    Gregg Pascoe

Steve Haralampu

Clark Hodder

Andrea Howard

David Janszen

Judy Kaplan

Jim King

Betty Mahoney

Rob Malenka

Harold Masters

Roy McDonald

Deborah McGrath

Ronald Meehan

John Norton

Sue Oberbeck

Clarence Poisson

Jamie Radner

Steve Rosales

Leslie Ryan

Ed Rynne

Amy Shapiro

Elaine Shortell

Andrea Torrielli and Dave
    Goguen

Vivian Vasil

A wordsmith's keen indebtedness to some Smithies:

Carmen Aleman

Susan Heuck Allen

Jane and Dave Barry

Lucinda and Wesley Brown

Nina Cuccio

Paula DeGiacomo

Maria Del Rio

Odette Fields and Jay
    Newsome

Iris Brass Goldstein

Joan Graham
Jennifer Green
Delia Guazzo
Barbara and John Hill
Mary Ann Hilles and Troy
   Squires
Tanya Kucherov
Barbara Oakes

Dianne Okolo and Paul
   Fanelli
Lori Blount Radford
Cynthia Rallis
Robin Rose
Hilary Shor
Linda Denney Wagner

And to all those who saw what it took to write this book, much obliged.

Joseph Agosto
Roberta Alessandra
Luis Alvarez
Arthur Anders
Matthew Antonellis
Marcy Bajusz
Robin Goldner Banning
Ettel Bar-Or
Steve Becker
Angelina Bencivenga
Betty Bernstein
Alaina Bixon
Alissa Bixon
Ronda Bixon
Kylie Blackman
Christine and Mitch Bosse
Jan Thaw and Richard Bruce
Rodica Candea
Anita Carmine
Catherine Colletta
Meghan Cruz
Joseph Cunningham
Dino Dal Pozzol
Patty Dann

Marty and Susan Danoff
Frank Dardeno
Nancy Davis
Robin Desmet
Frank Didik
Julia D'Orazio
Eleanor Eastman
Travis Evans
Roger and Patricia Favale
Maria Flores
Judith Kessler and Robert
   Froehlich
Nina Gaffny
Ralph Galen
Merle Glenn
Barbara Glickman
Paula Glickman
Rena Glickman
Joan Durga Glaser Goldberg
Steve Goldberg
Miriam Gomez
Pascale Gousseland
Elinor Greenberg
Steve Gruber

Rui Guerreiro

David Gumpert

Yolette Cetoute Hansen

Nina Haritos

Daniel Ishmael

Margie Israel

Evie Ivy

Toy Tsuya and David Kahane

Brian Keeler

Alexis Kirk

Isabel Komar

Freya Koss

Elsa Hidalgo Latheef

Herve Lequitte

Jeff Levy

Jane Lewis

WenWen Lin

Bill Lindauer

Laura Lonshein Ludwig

Patricia Manthorne

Camden Melendy

Dr. Avner Molcho

Barbra Music

Wendy Nan Rees

Chicky Newman

Kevin O'Connor

Rich Padova

Bobby Perel

Belinda Plutz

Carlos Pujols

Linda Rand

Harry Rivera

Joe and Nancy Salah

Brigitte Salvador

Anita Sanz

Gail Saraf

Darius Schmidt

Joan Schwarz

Parimal Shah

Conrad Sharpe

Antonia Shelzi

John Shelzi

Marc Shenfield

Dr. Ram Kumar Shrivastava

Dr. H. Blair Simpson

Sue Sirois

Barbara Skala

Pat Rupe and Michael Smith

Richard Spain

Judy Starr

Charles Stewart

Chris Sweetnam

Julia Szabo

Norm Tauber and Judy Teller

Luke Terry

Clare Shelzi Thompson

Natella Vaidman

Phil Vanaria

Diane West

John Richard Wheelen

Jimmy Wilcox

Frank Williams

Dr. Ron Winchel

Paula Wisnik

Hugs to Kittery, Larry, Lucky, Owly, and Tidbit for their Purring Committee.

ABOUT ATMOSPHERE PRESS

Atmosphere Press is an independent, full-service publisher for excellent books in all genres and for all audiences. Learn more about what we do at atmospherepress.com.

We encourage you to check out some of Atmosphere's latest releases, which are available at Amazon.com and via order from your local bookstore:

Finding Us, by Kristin Rehkamp

The Ideological and Political System of Banselism, by Royard Halmonet Vantion (Ancheng Wang)

Unconditional: Loving and Losing an Addict, by Lizzy and Adam

Telling Tales and Sharing Secrets, by Jackie Collins, Diana Kinared, and Sally Showalter

Nursing Homes: A Missionary's Journey Through Heaven's Waiting Room, by Tim Eatman Ph.D.

Timeline of Stars, by Joe Adcock

A Boy Who Loved Me, by Wilson Semitti

The Injustice in Justice, by Charmaine Loverin

Living in the Gray, by Katie Weber

Living with Veracity, Dying with Dignity, by Alison Clay-Duboff

Noah's Rejects, by Rob Kagan

A lot of Questions (with no answers)?, by Jordan Neben

Cowboy from Prague: An Immigrant's Pursuit of the American Dream, by Charles Ota Heller

Sleeping Under the Bridge, by Melissa Baker

The Only Prayer I Ever Have to Say Is Thank You, by M. Kaya Hill

Amygdala Blue, by Paul Lomax

A Caregiver's Love Story, by Nancie Wiseman Attwater

ABOUT THE AUTHOR

If there's an afterlife, how 'bout a better deal?

Blair Sorrel is an open book and a cautionary tale. In spite of her disability, she managed stints as *Free Time's* "Dollarwise Dilettante" columnist, Together Dating Service's matchmaker, and New York Blood Services' apheresis recruiter.

Blair also worked as the founder of StreetZaps, a stray voltage clearinghouse that the National Electric Code showcased sporadically, Con Edison and the Electric Power and Research Institute respected, Channel 11/WPIX featured, and that former Las Vegas Mayor Oscar Goodman made an official public service.

She was the first community representative that Con Edison ever invited to their annual Jodie S. Lane Stray Voltage Detection, Mitigation, and Prevention National Conference starting in 2008.

It is said there are born writers. Wet behind the ears left the womb with a greeting card in one diminutive paw and a ballpoint pen in the other, now the big baby strives to enlarge her readership. A scribbler with arrested development and decidedly anti-social, Blair would nonetheless give you the shirt off her back were she not so modest. Her Ladyship remains a true altruist and a lifelong animal lover.

Printed in the USA
CPSIA information can be obtained
at www.ICGtesting.com
CBHW021841291223
3026CB00005B/23